Satchel Paige's America

Satchel Paige's America

WILLIAM PRICE FOX

THE UNIVERSITY OF ALABAMA PRESS • TUSCALOOSA

Designer: Michele Myatt Quinn
Typeface: Bembo

The paper on which this book is printed meets the minimum
requirements of American National Standard for Information
Science—Permanence of Paper for Printed Library Materials,
ANSI Z39.48–1984.

Frontispiece: *Satchel Paige* by Arthur K. Miller. Used by per-
mission.

Library of Congress Cataloging-in-Publication Data

Fox, William Price.
    Satchel Paige's America / William Price Fox.
        p.   cm.
    "Fire Ant books."
    ISBN 0-8173-5189-2 (pbk. : alk. paper)
    1. Paige, Satchel, 1916–1982—Miscellanea. 2. Baseball
players—United States—Biography. I. Title.
    GV865.P3F69 2005
    796.357'092—dc22   2004018911

Satchel Paige's America

Left to right: Sportswriter William Price Fox meets with Satchel Paige and sports editor Jay Cee Bee at the Twilight Zone Lounge of the Rhythm Lanes Bowling Alley, ca. 1970s, to gather material for his book on Satchel Paige (photograph from *The [Kansas City] Call)*

CHAPTER

THE FIRST TIME I met Satchel Paige he was drinking beer in the Twilight Zone Lounge of the Rhythm Lanes Bowling Alley in Kansas City. The first thing he wanted to know was, was I on an expense account. I said I was, and he hooked his head and signaled the bartender for another round. Satch's second question, "Where you from, Bo?" From then on he called me Bo.

"South Carolina. Columbia, South Carolina. But I'm working out in L.A. right now."

Jay Cee Bee, the editor of the *Kansas City Call*, had taken me out to see him and told him I was doing an article for *Holiday Magazine*. Jay Cee had brought along a photographer.

"Columbia! I'll be dogged. That's a fine town. Fine town. Hell, I was arrested there last year. Well not exactly arrested, I was, you know, stopped. My back springs were riding low and they thought I was carrying whiskey. So they pulled me over just as I was getting ready to cross a bridge over a pretty good size river."

He grinned and a gold tooth flashed. "I showed them my driver's license and one of my eight-by-tens and they like to fell out. I wound up signing about nine or ten, you know, to this guy or that gal, things like that. Those boys were so happy they gave me a three- or four-motorcycle escort over the bridge and on out to the road to Atlanta. I'm telling you they treated me like I was some kind of royalty."

He pushed his porkpie hat to the back of his head and drained his glass. As he signaled for another round I knew one thing for sure, it wasn't going to be any trouble getting him to talk. "Yeah, that was it, I was heading for Atlanta. Now that ain't a bad town either. Nosir. I had me some great times in that old burg. Great times. Fine clubs down there and that food is A-number one. It can't be beat. Hey, I'll tell you who lives there right this second, Henry Aaron." He held up two fingers side by side, "That's us, me and Hank, we're just like that."

I told him he'd been stopped at the Gervais Street Bridge and how this was the bridge the bootleggers used to use to take whiskey over to Georgia. "A Columbia cop sees those springs riding low like that and they'll pull you over every time."

He said he had friends who made moonshine back in Alabama who used heavy-duty springs and when the car was loaded up the trunk stayed level. "Only problem was when it wasn't loaded down that thing stuck up like one of those old long-legged Texas jackrabbits."

I let him know that that was an old trick. Then I told him about how my dad and uncle ran a Georgia stream still back in the forties that made twelve hundred gallons a day.

He leaned forward with both elbows on the table with a string of fast questions—he figured I was lying. "Hey now, how'd they get power out there to run a thing like that?"

"Hooked up a Delco Plant to a Ford engine. They ran it all night; they had to have juice for the lights."

"Twelve hundred gallons." He began drumming his long fingers on the table—he still didn't believe me. "How high was that mash feeder?"

"Twenty to twenty-two feet."

"How much sugar to how much meal?"

"Two-thirds sugar, one-third meal."

He wasn't letting up. "How much he sell it for?"

"Three dollars a gallon. Anything else?"

"Hold it, hold the phone right there. I happen to know for a fact that the feds keep a pretty sharp eye on people buying that much sugar." He laced his fingers together and, in a gesture I would see over and over again, slid them behind his head and smiled. "Now how'd they get around that one?"

I told him it had been a problem and how they'd bought three or four boxcars of Southern Bakery Four Count Cinnamon Rolls and how they sat out in the woods on straight chairs and unwrapped them and tossed them in the slurry.

Satch slapped both hands flat on the table laughing. "Bo, that is great. I'm sure as hell going to spread this one around. That's the best I've ever heard. Now let me tell you something not many people know about. You get you some good corn whiskey—I mean stuff that's made with a lot of meal and not loaded down with too much sugar—and you put a little age on that stuff and it'll smooth down as smooth as anything Mister Johnny Walker ever put on the shelf. Red Label or your Black Label."

I hung in there and told him the best way to age corn was in an old-fashioned fifty-five-gallon Coca-Cola syrup barrel. "See, the syrup gives it that red brown color you want and that old oak is the best thing in the world for ageing."

He made a church steeple with his fingers and cut his eyes at me. "Bo, you know some shit about whiskey, don't you?"

"I should, it runs in the family."

Jay Cee Bee motioned for his photographer to move in and get a shot of us laughing but Satch waved him off. "Dammit, Jay Cee, I told you I didn't want no pictures. Now get him on out of here."

"Oh hell, Satch. Let him get something."

"No, I don't want no shots of me in no damn bar and you know it."

Jay Cee waved the photographer away and, mumbling to himself, hooked back in over his beer.

The Twilight Zone Lounge has a long bar running the

length of the room with a big blue mirror centered in the middle of the back bar. Red leatherette booths line the walls, and a rainbow-colored Wurlitzer, loaded down with Ray Charles, Lou Rawls, and Al Hibbler, never stopped playing. Down on one end of the bar four beer drinkers were arguing about what round Ezzard Charles stopped Joe Louis. Suddenly the bartender shouted, "All right! All right now! Ease it up. You're getting too damn loud in here."

He slapped a dime on the bar. "Call the *Star* and find out; y'all are driving me crazy."

A tall man with his left arm in a sling was taking money out of his wallet with one hand and laying it on the bar. "Here's twenty bucks. Saying it was the twelfth."

Down the bar a hand went up. "Give me ten of that."

Satch stood up and raised his glass for attention. "Man put your money back in your pocket! Buy your kids some shoes!"

The room looked over and Satch took over. "It was the twelfth. Hell, any fool off the street will tell you that."

The man stacked his bills, then tapping them on the counter he looked around the room. "How about Billy Conn? Any bets on how long he lasted?"

Satch was still on his feet. "Listen here! I saw that fight! Saw it in Madison Square Garden, New York City. I was right there. Front row center. You check the newsreels. You check the magazines. You'll see me there, right up front."

His big voice drowned out Ray Charles singing "Georgia." "Joe caught him in the thirteenth. Caught him in the corner and nailed him on the ropes. I was looking straight up at him when he put him away. Hell, that wasn't no fight, I don't care what they say."

Satch put his glass down and stuck out his long left arm. He began jabbing the air. "Billy Conn would peck at him like a chicken and back up on his bicycle. Peck and run."

He jabbed three or four more times. "Peck and run. Peck and run." Satch finished off the flurry with a nifty little hook. "That's all he knew how to do. Looked like a little banty rooster worrying a bulldog. But Joe kept after him and caught his ass. Put him away. I mean clean away. That's when they came up with the saying, he can run but he can't hide" He said it again louder, making sure everyone heard it, "Yessir, he can run but he can't hide."

Satch sat back down, finished his beer, and shook a Marlboro out of a hard pack. Jay Cee Bee, who had been waiting for him and the room to settle down, reached over and lit it with his Zippo. "Satchel," he wanted to get the interview back on a higher lever for his paper. "What do you consider to be your greatest contribution to baseball?" He sat back pleased with himself and the question.

Satch frowned and with his little finger picked a piece of tobacco from his tongue. "Shee-it, Jay Cee, what kind of question is that? Why don't you go on home and let me and Bo here do some talking?"

"But I just wanted him to have something to write about."

Satch made a circle in the air with his finger for another round. "Don't you worry about these old mules. Me and Bo here have plenty to talk about. Now you just go on home and leave us alone."

Jay Cee Bee and his photographer left and Satch said, "OK, now what do you want to talk about?"

I'd only seen him pitch once in an exhibition back in Columbia. "Why don't you tell me how you pitched to a few of the big names in the majors."

"OK, fire away. I'll see what I can do."

"All right, let's start with Mantle. I always liked him."

"Mickey! Hell, I remember the first time I faced that boy like it was yesterday. Had some fun off him too. What I did was I gave him my old hesitation pitch and I'll be dogged if he didn't swing before the ball left my hand. Then when I let the ball go, he swung again and missed. Struck at it twice. I hollered in at the ump that that should have been two strikes."

"You've got to be kidding."

"If I'm lying, I'm dying. I swear it. That's how fast that boy was. Lord, he was fast. I'm going to tell you something right here and you be sure and write it up. Mickey could have batted five hundred just laying down bunts from the left side. You give him that extra step and no one could touch him. Pitchers couldn't move fast enough, and there ain't a third baseman alive that's fool enough to crowd in on him."

The label on his bottle was wet and he began picking it off. "First time he bunted on me, I sprang out toward the third base line, picked it up and whipped it over. See, I used to throw it from a low crouch. Hell, I still do. I don't straighten up, just throw it from where I pick it up. Anyhow, I whipped it over and hell, what you talking about, that man had already passed the bag and was cruising back wiping the sweat out of his cap.

"Mickey was something, all right. Lord, as a rookie there never was a man like that. I tell you what, if it hadn't been for his knees and all those operations he'd have been the greatest ever. And he was strong. He hit that clock in Comiskey Park. Ain't nobody ever done that. Yessir, he was a number one player batting, fielding, and running. You ever see him run? Had that smooth power; had that low running. Head stayed so smooth it looked like he was riding a bicycle. You could put a glass of iced tea on it and he wouldn't spill a drop. But, pod-ner, he was flying. I mean flying. And he was a fine boy too. Fine. Everybody like old Mickey. Hell, I've seen him stand out in the rain with water running down his nose signing autographs. Not many players will do that. He'd be out there signing matchbooks and napkins. You know how little kids are, they'll use anything they pick up, hell they'll even use toilet paper. Now that's enough Mickey for a while. Who else you want to talk about?"

"How about DiMaggio?"

"Well, let me see here. I guess I first met up with Joe out on the coast. Yeah, he was playing for the San Francisco Seals. Now here's the story on Joe. See, he'd hit flat-footed, and he always kept jangling around on you keeping loose. When you're as loose as Joe you don't get set and you can hit anyone. And he was doing it, pod-ner. He was doing it. But I knew how to get to him. Anyhow, one day he comes up to me and says, 'Satch, the scouts are here today and watching me, so I'm going to have to hit you.'

"Well I figured the scouts were watching me too. So I told him. 'OK, Joe, if you can see it you go ahead and hit it.' See, I had my number one control going and I had my Stinger ready any time I needed it. So I just knew I could get everything by him. Anyhow, I struck him out in the first, then I think I got him again in the fourth. Along about the seventh he nipped me for a single. Then in the ninth I got him to pop up. And right in there was when the Yankee scouts sent that telegram that said, 'Joe hit Satch one for four. He's ready to play for us.' Somebody sent me a copy of that thing. When we get out to the house I'll show it to you."

He sipped his beer and wiped the foam from his mouth with the back of his hand. "Listen here now. I don't want you writing anything about me drinking or smoking. See, I work with the kids out in the parks. And you know how it is. I don't want them seeing me with the brew. No brew, and no cigarettes; I don't care how broke I get, you'll never see me advertising stuff like that. It breaks the kids down before they hit their growth."

"Fair enough. You got a deal."

"OK, now I'll tell you a little something else about Joe. That old boy took a full cut at that ball, and when I say full cut, that's what I mean, a full cut. Look at the pictures of him when he swings and check his shirt across the back. He stretches it tighter than a drumhead. Go on check it out, you don't have to take my word for it. When he swung there wasn't a wrinkle in that thing. Looked like a Chinaman just ironed it."

The man with his arm in a sling came over to the booth and Satch cocked his head. "Yessir, what can we do for you?"

"I want to know how I can check the newsreels to see if you sat in the front row for that Billy Conn fight."

Satch laughed but kept checking him out looking for the sarcasm. "Man, now how in the hell would I know something like that? Call up your senator. Call up your congressman." He called out to the bartender, "Roscoe, give this man the phone book, he wants to look up his congressman."

The man didn't find it funny. "Well what magazines were you talking about then? I'm going to check up on this."

Satch's eyes narrowed. "Hell man all the big ones. *Life. Look. . . . Saturday Evening Post.* Hey! Hold it a minute here. I don't care for you coming over here like this and interrupting a private conversation and asking me to account to you. Now why don't you just get the hell on out of here and leave us alone."

The man saw the wind picking up. "I didn't mean no harm. I declare I didn't."

Satch said, "Well you just keep on moving. OK?"

"OK, Satch."

Satch watched the man go back to the bar. "Now why in the hell did he want to come over and bother us like that? People are getting crazier every day." He was upset for about three seconds, then it passed and was over. "OK now, who else you want to talk about?"

"How about Ted Williams."

"Williams?" He was stalling so he could think.

"Yeah, Williams."

"Low." I've never heard *low* sound so low. "Low and outside. Up in here." He drew his forefinger across his chest, "Shame on you." He dragged "shame" out, letting it hang in the air, and you could hear the ball buzzing by.

"The onliest way to pitch a man like that is as low and as outside as you can get it. You want him reaching out, way the hell out. What you're trying to do is keep him off balance. And that was hard with Mr. Theodore Williams. He was one hard bird to pitch to. Hard, I'm talking hard."

Satch ticked his teeth on the rim of his glass and reached back fifteen or twenty years. "Bo, I've seen him take one way out on the outside corner and pull that thing clean over the right field wall. That's how strong and quick he was. And I'll tell you something else about him not many people know about: You had to be careful and protect yourself when you pitched him. You had to make sure you hid that ball when you gripped it. See, he had those damn X-ray eyes that could see through a brick wall. Hell, I heard tell how he could take one look at a 78 record spinning around and he could call out the title and the singer and the day it was cut.

"Anyhow he'd catch you wrapping that ball, you know down the seams or across them, and when he picked that up and knew what was coming, church was out. Church was clean out. Because that bird knew what you were throwing before you turned it loose. Hell, a lot of times he'd know what you were throwing before you did. And if you figuring on getting a fastball by him, you can just forget it. You know how they say getting a fastball by Henry Aaron is like getting the sun by a rooster? That's the exact same thing it was with Ted. Only worse, because the faster you throw it the harder he hits it. . . . You heard of the Boudreau Shift?"

"Yeah, I think so. But I never understood it."

He laughed, "Neither did old Boudreau. Now you talk about a total dyed-in-the-wool one-hundred-percent catastrophe, that was one from the beginning. See, Boudreau was managing the Indians and he thought he had Ted all figured out. What he did was move all his outfielders over to right field. He was figuring, I mean what he was trying to figure, was since Ted was going to pull it to the right he'd just load up the field and stop him. Hell, it didn't do a lick of good. All Ted did was knock it clean over their heads. Or if he took a notion, he'd punch it out to left field and then just ramble on down to first.

"Hell what you talking about, you try and figure out how to stop a man like Ted Williams and he'll give you a forty-day migraine. Maybe you'll come up with something eventually but by the time you do that man's done hit you for a hundred home runs. . . . If I had to take my pick of the greatest hitters of all times I'd say Ted Williams and Josh Gibson, hands down and side by side. But Ted could cold hit that ball hard. Hard. I'm talking hard. He hit it so hard it would tear the glove right off a first baseman."

He lit a cigarette, took a long drag and spoke through the smoke. "Of course he lost his best years when he went in the service. But that was all right too. You can't fault him for that. I heard he was a good pilot too. A Marine pilot, they were the best."

Satch continued. "What did he bat in forty-one anyway? Four oh five? Four oh six? Something like that. And yeah, he had close to four hundred the year before that. Ted Williams, yeah, he was something else. There won't be many ballplayers like him. Not around here there won't."

It was at this point I made a decision. "Satch, there's something we've got to talk about. And it's just a little bit delicate."

"Well, let's hear it."

An old ballplayer out in L.A. had told me that most of the writers and producers who'd worked with Satch had promised to make him some money and almost none of them had come through. I said, "I'm getting four thousand dollars for this piece. But since you're going to be doing all the talking and all I'm going to be doing is writing it down, I'm going to split it with you right down the middle."

I pulled out ten one hundred dollar bills I'd folded together. "Here's a thousand. I'll give you the rest when we finish."

"Well, well now." He was beaming. "Thank you, Bo. This is mighty nice. I can sure as hell use it." He flipped through the bills and slid them in his shirt pocket. Then he said, "What you're saying is if you give it all to me now I might vanish in the night. Is that right?"

"Or you might get lockjaw."

He laughed, "No, no danger of that. They don't call me Motor Mouth for nothing." He raised his hand and Rudolph came out from behind the bar. Satch handed him a hundred, "I want to square up my bar bill. This cover it?"

Rudolph said, "Sure Satch, and you got some change coming."

I interrupted. "No, let me do this. I need a receipt. OK?"

Rudolph said, "Fine, fine with me. Shall I write anything on it?"

"Yeah, let's see. Just say "Paige Party," that'll do it."

Rudolph hooked his head, "No problem. No problem at all."

"Bo," Satch soft-punched my shoulder. "Me and you are going to get along just fine."

"OK. Now how about telling me some more about Boudreau?"

"Hell yeah. I'll tell you anything you want to know and then some. OK, when I came up with the Indians in forty-eight Boudreau was the manager and Bill Veeck was the owner. See, Veeck brought me up, but it was Boudreau who sort of looked out after me out on the field. He let me do things the way I was used to doing them, and he wouldn't let Bill Veeck mess me up with something new.

"Here, I'll give you a good example on that one. See, I have me this move on bunts that no one had and they claim no one ever has had. It was like I told you about Mickey. What I'd do was when that ball went down the third base line I'd get over and scoop it up and throw to first while I was still crouching over. Not many men can do that, especially when you're over forty, they can't get enough stuff on it. But Bill Veeck would shout out, 'Satch, we're playing against the Yankees, we're in the damn pennant race. Ain't it too late to be pulling some crazy damn thing like that? Ain't you got some better way of throwing it over?'

"And Boudreau would jump up out of the dugout hollering his head off. 'Veeck! Damn your sorry-assed soul; you leave that man alone. He's been doing that for thirty years, what in the hell can we be teaching him now.' And then he'd holler at me, 'Satch, don't you listen to that fool. You do things the way you want to do them. I'll take care of Mister Veeck.' You know old Boudreau was a red-hot shortstop himself; he knew all about fielding bunts. Yeah Boudreau, for a manager, he wasn't too bad. Matter of fact when I came up in forty-eight he was leading both leagues in batting. You check that one out. I can cold guarantee it was a flat four hundred."

The Happy Hour was on—two drinks for the price of

one—and the crowd was packed in up at the bar. Nat King Cole was easing into "Mona Lisa" when I asked Satch to tell me what it was like playing in the 1948 pennant race.

His face dropped and he looked at me with true disappointment. "Bo, what kind of question is that?" He laid his hand on my arm. "You ought to know better than that. It wasn't like anything before or after. That's the kind of thing you just can't compare to anything out there."

"I'm sorry."

"That's all right." He lit a cigarette and shook out the match. "You know, if I had to pick out what was the biggest scrape I'd ever been in in baseball I'd have to say it was right in there. Man, it was tight. I mean tight. That's why it wasn't like anything else. See, I'd just joined the Indians and we were tied with the Yankees for first place. I mean things were so tight you couldn't drive a nail through them. But I had my Stinger going, and I had that number one control, so old Veeck and Boudreau kept holding me out for the last couple innings so I could do the closing.

"But that one time I'm thinking about right now was when we were in the ninth and we were tied and the bases were loaded and there were no outs and here comes the middle of the Yankees' batting order. And right in here, they send me in. I'm telling you when I walked out to that mound and knew I had to face Mickey Mantle and then Joe DiMaggio and then Charlie Keller I could feel that cold sweat just running down my back.

"I tried to whistle to calm down but my lips were as dry as sandpaper. I could have struck a match on them. I mean I didn't have a drop of moisture on me.

"See, all they had to do was hit just about anything and it was all over. All I had to do was walk one, or let them bunt one, or hit a sacrifice fly, or even a ground ball and they had the game. I mean anything I did that was even close to wrong and it was all over.

"Well, I struck out Mantle and I got Joe to pop up. Then

after I took a couple long deep breaths, and made sure I wasn't looking over to see Bill Veeck or Lou Boudreau going crazy in the dugout, I threw three fast ones right by Charlie Keller. Bo, right in there was where we won that pennant. And you talk about three happy people, one of them was Bill Veeck, and one of them was Lou Boudreau, and one of them is sitting right here in front of you and that was yours truly. Me.

"Later on I asked Bill Veeck why he waited so long to put me in there? And he said he was so scared he didn't know what to do himself. He said he knew he could get one good inning out of me and he was waiting for that right minute. And I said, 'Well you sure as hell waited long enough.'

"And he said, 'Well Satch, you saved it for us. And I'm not ever going to forget it.'"

Satch raised his hand and hollered out. "Hey Rudolph! It's like a funeral parlor in here. How 'bout some music?"

"Coming up."

In a minute the jukebox was playing "Up on the Roof," and Satch began doing long hand pulls and snapping his fingers with the rhythm. "I've heard that song a hundred times. And I could hear it a hundred more. Fine song. Fine. What kind of music you like, Bo?"

I said, "Rhythm and blues, jazz, country and western."

"Same here. I like everything. I don't think I could have made it driving all those long trips without my radio and my guitar. And hell, I even play a Jew's harp. Matter of fact I carry an extra transistor radio in case my car one goes out on me. Music, that's something I've got to have with me at all times."

I asked if Casey Stengel was coaching the Yankees the year the Indians won the pennant. Satch said, "You better believe it. And he was a helluva coach. But I'll tell you something. I used to drive that old boy crazy. Pure T-crazy. It would get to be the seventh inning and he'd get up and start humping up and down in front of the dugout spitting and kicking the dirt and carrying on. You know how he is.

"An' he'd be yelling." Satch's voice went high and scratchy—

he was sounding like Stengel, exactly like Stengel. "'OK now boys, it's the seventh inning and I wants you to get me them hits now. I mean now! I want them hits now. Because if you don't get them you know what's going to happen in the ninth? They're going to put in old Father Time'—see, that's what he called me Father Time—'and he ain't going to give you nothing. He ain't got but one pitch but that's all he needs because you ain't going to be seeing it and if you can't see it, you sure as hell ain't going to be hitting it.'

"He'd keep walking up and down, up and down, all crouched over and humped over like a chicken scratching after corn and clacking. I mean he looked like a chicken; he walked like a chicken; and I'll be damned if he didn't sound like a chicken. 'Come on now get me them hits. Get me them hits.'"

He shook his head smiling. "Yeah, old Casey, he was a mess. There won't be another one like that out there; they made him and then they broke the mold. I mean it, there will never be another Casey Stengel."

Satch pointed his nose at my beer. "Bo, you hungry? I'm coming up on starving. Come on, drink that down, I'm going to take you over to Gates's Place. They've got a barbecue over there that's so good it'll knock you flat on your back. People come here from everywhere for it. Hell, they come in here all the way from Des Moines, Iowa, and Peoria, Illinois, and those are both pretty damn good drives."

CHAPTER  2

ALL THE WAY across town, heading for Gates's, Satch kept changing lanes passing every car he saw and punching in different radio stations. He finally picked up Lou Rawls coming in from St. Louis. "Old Lou sings a song and that thing stays sung. Once he puts his stamp on it no one can touch it. I caught his show a couple times in L.A. last year and we had a couple brews between the sets." We were in a thirty-five-mile zone and Satch was doing a flat sixty. "All I had to do was name a song and he'd do it. Now that's one boy that knows how to entertain."

Gates's Place was big, well lighted, clean, and packed. The minute we walked in everyone seated and everyone behind the counter waved and shouted Satch's name. One guy sang out, "Here he is folks, the great Satchel Paige." Satch aimed a pistol finger and fired it. "Hey there, Lonnie, long time no see."

Gates himself left the steam table and came out drying his hands on his apron to shake. "Where you been boy? We been missing you." Satch shook hands with one hand and waved to the room with the other. Then he slapped me on the back. "Listen here Bo, when you write this piece up you be sure and mention my buddy Gates here. This is the number one best barbecue in the country and it's right here in town. That right, Gates?"

"That's right, Satch."

We stood there and Old Motor Mouth was off and running on about barbecue. "No lie, them cooks up north and back east they don't know what they're doing with barbecue. Hell, anything they put a little smoke to they call it barbecue. And then they drench it down with some ketchup-based mess." He looped his arm around Gates's shoulders. "But my boy here, he knows exactly what he's doing. And let me tell you something else, right here and right now, I've eaten barbecue in almost every state in the United States and Canada and Mexico and as far down as Cuba and South America, and right here is the best of the best. Gates in my book is the numero uno. And listen, Bo, you be sure and mention that he has been internationally recommended by none other that Mister Duncan Hines himself and he's got the plaque to prove it."

Satch ordered barbecued lamb; I went for the pork. When it was served and Satch reached for the bill Gates picked it up and tore it in half, then in half again. "Satch, you know your money ain't no good in here. How come you want to embarrass me like this."

Satch hooked his head, "Well, we thank you, old man. I appreciate this, I swear I do."

Gates motioned for one of his help to come over. "Joseph, I want you to make up a bag of cues for Satch here to take home. And put in plenty of cole slaw, Lahoma likes that stuff. Right, Satch?"

"You right about that."

Satch insisted we have lemonade with the barbecue. "Most folks drink beer with their cues and they wind up ruining it. It just ain't the same; lemonade brings out the flavor better. Then you got some folks that like it with iced tea, but me, I always go for ice-cold strong lemonade." As he held forth about how to pick out lemons and shave the ice for the lemonade, I knew if I mentioned coffee or Norwegian salmon or toilet paper he would be right at home and off and running. No, there wasn't going to be any trouble getting Satchel Paige to talk. The problem was how to rein him in and keep it on baseball.

We each had two sandwiches before Satch leaned his chair back against the wall with his hands behind his head. "You get down in Texas and they barbecue beef and they start carrying on about how wonderful it is. But you know something, that ain't barbecue, that ain't even close to barbecue and I'm going to tell you why. You go out back here and you'll see three or four cords of hickory stacked up. See, you got to have hickory for barbecuing because it burns slower and you want that smoke getting inside your meat. And I'll tell you something else, what you want is your green hickory—see that burns even slower and it puts out the best smoke in the world. Down in Texas they use mesquite and oak because they don't have hickory. As far as I'm concerned, and you can write this down as a natural fact, you can have the finest pork or beef or whatever you're using but without hickory wood you cannot have barbecue. And that, old buddy, is the long and the short of it. Now I guess they can call it barbecue because it's a free country and you can call anything you want anything you want. But as far as this old boy is concerned when I get to Texas I stick with cheeseburgers."

I asked him about the story going around that he never ate anything fried, meat or anything fried.

He winced, closed his eyes, and shook his head. It was a sore subject. "Bo, you got to realize there ain't but a few things in the papers and the magazines they get right. Maybe they get the weddings right and once in a while the obituaries. But most of the time they're so far off base it ain't even funny. Now that story about me and fried foods, that was one pack of lies from the goddamn beginning. Them reporters write anything that comes in their heads. And then every one of them copies the last one and it just gets bigger and bigger and before you know it it's clear out of control.

"Hell, they even make up words that I was saying. And rules I had to live by. Hell, they even had me on some crazy-assed diet. Said I didn't eat fried foods because it 'angrifies' the blood. What in the hell kind of word is 'angrify'? I may be a lot of things and I may not have gone to too much school but I sure as hell ain't stupid. I met up with the reporter who got that stuff started about me and I cussed him out real good. Right away he starts smiling and backing down saying how he and his editor were just having them some fun and how everybody loved it and how they didn't mean any harm. But I didn't give him one damn inch. I told him, yeah my wife and my kids read them funny things and they sure as hell didn't think they were funny.

"The guy said, 'Well, Satch, what can I do to help smooth it out?'

"And I said, 'Well to begin with you can write Lahoma a letter and she can show it to the kids and you tell her you were sorry. And then you can print a retraction about it in that sorry-assed paper of yours.' I don't get mad too much but boy, that stuff really got to me. But you know what that guy did? Nothing, not one damn thing.

"Bo, let me ask you something. How'm I going to eat eggs in the morning when I'm out on the road unless I fry them? I sure as hell ain't going to suck them. And how about bacon? And how about ham? And how about sausage? What am I going to do with stuff like that? Here I am on some old sorry-assed gravel road four hundred miles from nowhere, what kind of breakfast can I cook on my Coleman if I can't fry me up something?

"Maybe them reporters figure I eat some Corn Flakes or some Rice Krispies, you know snap, crackle, and pop. Yeah, yeah, that would do it. A nice bowl of Rice Krispies, then maybe I could put on some berries. Strawberries might be in season and that would be nice too. . . . And yeah, maybe a little skim milk to keep down the fat. See that would be good for that diet they were telling everyone I was on. I ain't ever been on no goddamn diet. OK, so I eat those Rice Krispies and berries and skim milk." He laughed, "I get hungry just thinking about how wonderful that would be out on the road when it's cold and maybe there's a little rain whistling down my ass. Then after a couple bowls, I climb back in my wagon and drive four hundred miles to the next town and when I get there I've got to get out with my glove on because I got to start throwing. Yessir-ee, them Rice Krispies, with their snap, crackle, and pop, would fix me up just about right. Maybe they figure I stop along the road and get me a couple slices of bologna and a can of Vienna Sausage and some light bread.

"Bo, if I didn't have time to stop on the side of the road and set up my Coleman and fry something I'd stop at a hamburger joint and get me three or four cheeseburgers and a couple Orange Crushes. And I'd finish that off with a Mister Goodbar. That was always good. See, back in the thirties and forties and up into the fifties you could get you a cheeseburger with lettuce and tomatoes with a big slice of onion on a toasted bun with a pickle chip on top all for a dime. Hell, today all you can do with a dime is weigh yourself and they don't even give you your fortune.

"And that Mister Goodbar was good too. All it was was chocolate and peanuts, but man it was good. Back then it was only a nickel and it was as big as a license plate. A few years back they shrank it down and jacked up the price to fifteen cents. It's up to twenty now and still going up. But I still buy them and my kids love them. I wish I'd saved one of those old ones so I could show them how big that thing used to be.

"Listen Bo, you write this down and you get it straight. I want the people out there to know something and this time I want it straight. I eat fried eggs. And I eat fried bacon. And I eat fried ham and fried sausage and fried everything. And anytime I got enough time and enough grease, I'm frying me up some chicken and some hoe cake. You ever eat fried hoe cake? Ain't nothing like it."

I said, "Hell, I even like hush puppies."

"Hush puppies. Man, what you talking about. You could squeeze the grease out of a batch of those babies and you'd have enough to take care of a full-size Buick. But you know something, when you're putting in the kind of day I'm putting in and all that driving and all that pressure, a man needs all the grease he can handle. You write this down too, ain't nothing wrong with grease. Not one thing. You get right down to it there ain't nothing better to cook with, especially chicken and pork chops. Man, you put your pork chops in an oven and I don't care how much you surround them with pineapples and cherries and orange slices and pieces of parsley and stuff like that, they still can't touch a pork chop fried in plain old hard lard. I mean you take your collards or your mustard greens, that stuff wouldn't be fit to eat unless you put in a big spoon of ham grease and sprinkle on some vinegar. If I had to put my finger on why the South is so famous for it's food, I'd say the big secret is grease. That's right, grease. Hell, that's why a lot of people call the South the hard lard belt."

Satch said he was beginning to pace himself, and every now and then when he thinks of retirement he thinks of heading back down South. Back where he could have a garden and catch fish every day. "I'm what you call a fish demon. I'll fish sun or moon, rain or shine, it don't matter. Last time I went back to Mississippi me and Lahoma fished almost every day. She loves it too, so do the kids. We caught plenty of shrimps and prawns and crabs, plenty of bream and bass and redbreasts, plenty of everything—ain't no better eating fish in the world than that cold freshwater redbreast. He is the number one fish down there and you better believe it.

"I'll tell you something else and you can mark this down as a number one prediction. You give this country twenty or thirty more years to wake up and everybody that's got any sense is going to be living down South.

"Now you take it down there in the Carolinas, and over in Louisiana, and down into Florida. Why it's like a garden down there. That's where a man can live and not have to worry about where his next meal is coming from. Hell, you want to get yourself some fish, you just walk out your back door and stick your pole in the river and you got them. That's when they're good, when they're fresh like that and their eyes are shiny. You don't want to be messing with any cloudy-eyed fish. Those cloudy-eyeds will kill you quicker than a train, a guaranteed road direct to the graveyard.

"But say you want yourself some fresh vegetables, I don't mean this frozen mess they throwing at you nowadays, I said fresh vegetables. Like you want yourself some collards—you just go out in the backyard and just reach down and get them. Because they're right there. Then say you want some turnips or some rutabeggers with them collards, well you just reach down and scratch around and they're right there too. And maybe you got a bean vine whipping around your porch for some shade to keep the dogs cool. Why, you just reach out and pick them right there, pull off the strings, snap those babies in half, and slap them in the pot."

Satch was born and grew up in Mobile, Alabama, and whenever he gets nostalgic he says he thinks about the Gulf Coast. "Of course, you got to know what you're doing down there. You just can't go reaching under just any old rock or piece of sheet iron you see laying around because they got a couple snakes down there, they will get right with you. You take your moccasin, your cottonmouth moccasin, now he's bad. Bad. When he chomps down on you, you got yourself some trouble. And every evening just as the sun goes down, what you talking about, you can look out and see them cottonmouths swimming in like this," he held up all ten fingers, "and it looks like they're getting ready to invade the place. I mean there's so many you can't even count them. And they got a turtle down there, called the Blue. He's mean too. You go sticking your fingers near him and you ain't coming back with nothing. Nosir, he takes it all.

"Bo, I tell you what I used to do. I used to hang over them little bridges down there and smoke a couple cigarettes and look down in the water by the hour. I wasn't even fishing, I'd just be looking. I mean it, that's what I'd do. Man, you look down there long enough watching them big fish and sharks and turtles and big eels coming through and it'll make you stop and think. Hell, a lot of those operations don't even have any names.

"But even considering that and all the snakes and alligators, it's still the best place on earth to live. Like I said, ten and eleven months out of the year it's like a garden."

He laughed and shook his head. "We are playing ball down in Mississippi one time and I told one old boy from New York to watch out for Mister Cottonmouth Moccasin because that was one mean hombre. I told him first off he will stalk you till he gets close. Then when he gets you where he wants you, he'll wrap around your ankle to hold you still, and then he'll bite you. That fool believed every word and I had him so scared you'd see him walking down the middle of the road. See what I'm saying? He wasn't about to get close to any drain ditch. And he wasn't going near no kind of woods. Nosir, that boy was out in the middle and he was staying out in the middle. He was scared."

He talked on about growing up in Mobile and how his father was a professional gardener and how he was the sixth of eight children. Even when he was a kid of three or four he was already pitching because all day long he'd be throwing rocks at tin cans. "I'd do it by the hour. Do it till it was dark, then I'd go get under the streetlight and keep on throwing. I got so I couldn't miss. Hell, I could hit birds sitting on the wires, big ones and little ones, and I couldn't have been more than five or six. And you know something, I developed the same motion I still have. Slow and easy, that's the ticket. Never put too much pressure on anything. Just take a big windup and let it flow. Aiming takes care of itself. You know when you aim real hard at something, right there's your guaranteed way to miss. It tightens you up and things don't flow the way you want them. I learned real early to forget all that aiming business and just let it take care of itself. Because see, when you got that smooth motion going, that ball's going right where you want it, you don't have to lean on it. Now I'm not saying you don't pick out a spot. I'm saying something else. I'm saying that spot's there in your head all right but you just don't have to sweat it. Minute I see somebody aiming real hard, it can be a baseball, a football, a basketball, a golf shot, a pool shot, or anything, I'm betting good money they're going to miss it. I heard where some old golfer said when you putt you should try to be a little careless. Now that right there is some pretty good advice."

Satch was autographing menus for Gates when I asked him how often he pitched when he was barnstorming. Someone came by the table. "So long, Satch."

He reached up with his left hand and gave the man a high five. Then his eyes narrowed and he frowned at me. "Did you say *was*? Bo, what you talking about? Don't you be writing about no *was* with me. I'm getting ready to hit the road this week if I can get out of here. Hell, I got me five good men raring to go right his second."

I took the *was* out and asked him again. He said, "Now, that's better. I pitch every day and twice on Sunday if we got the crowd. And I mean every day. And I don't get all that rest those boys get in the majors on those featherbeds in those air-conditioned hotels. When I go to bed it's generally right there in my station wagon. . . . But I guess I've got to start facing it, I just ain't no spring chicken anymore. But you take me when I was going strong; I'd pitch doubleheaders, then drive three or four hundred miles, sleep in the car, and get up with my glove in my hand and pitch another full game. And if you don't think that will work on you and tear you down after a while you better back off. And I'll tell you something else, which they're just beginning to see in the majors, that night ball will chop your butt up into little pieces. See, it gets too cold out there on that mound and you never get a chance to stove up.

"But I don't want to sound like I'm complaining and I don't want you writing about me sounding like I'm complaining. I'm not the kind of guy who does much of that. I had me a great life and I'm going to keep on having it. It's like old Dizzy Gillespie says, 'You got to keep on with the keeping on.' Diz, that's another one of my best buddies. Hell, ain't he from South Carolina, down in there where you live?"

"You got it. He's from Cheraw, about ninety miles from Columbia."

"I thought so." Satch's elbows were on the table, his chin was in his fists. "Bo, you know something, a lot of times I go into the dressing room with a headache on account of all the money troubles I'd gotten myself in. Money, it's always money. Lord I could make it. But Lord, I could solid spend it too. Never could hold onto that old green. Stuff would go like it had wings. See, what I'm always doing is setting up the bar and loaning it out to boys I just met and boys I don't even know. See, I know where it goes but I just couldn't stop it. But the minute I get my uniform on and my socks and shoes fixed—"

He stopped and snapped his fingers. "Don't let me forget to tell you about my socks. Anyhow, like I was saying, the minute I get my uniform on, that headache is long gone. That's the way it is with me. That's the way it's always been. Then the minute I take it off, here she comes back—the troubles, the headaches, and the damn bills piling in in the mail. But it's like I said, you love something the way I love baseball and there ain't nothing going to bother you when you're playing. And that's the way it's been with me all my life."

I reminded him of his socks and he smiled, "OK, well it ain't no big secret but you might like to write about it. I guess my legs could be a little built up better. But they ain't and I'm stuck with them. So what I do is I'll slip on four or five pairs of stockings. See that way they look pretty good. And it's a lot warmer out there on the mound at night when that wind starts chipping away on you.

"Now I've got to tell you something else about socks before I forget it. You remember Bob Wills? Bob Wills and His Texas Playboys? See, I knew all those boys. Hell, I played a couple songs with them in the clubs. I'll tell you one right now that Bob Wills wrote. It's a country classic, 'San Antonio Rose.'

"Anyhow, one night old Bob had been hitting the jug pretty heavy and his boys had to dress him and push him out on the stage. Well sir, all the time they're playing Bob Wills keeps saying, 'Socks dammit, socks dammit,' like he was in real pain. And he was. Turned out they'd crammed his toes and feet down in his boots and they forgot to take out the damn socks."

After Satch autographed a few more menus for Gates to give to his customers, he stood up stretching. "I'd better get these old bones into bed before Lahoma comes looking for me. Tell you what, I'll take you out to the house while you're here. I've got a trunk full of clippings and pictures and some of the old posters we used to use. But tomorrow night I'm going to take you to one of the clubs I hang around where they got some music. And I'm going to tell you something else, you're going to see some dancing."

"Sounds even better."

"Yeah. Bo, you hang around a few more days and I'll give you a real story. I'll give you something to write about that no one has touched. Hey, something else, I want to thank you for the money. I know exactly where I'm going to use it."

CHAPTER  3

AFTER SATCH DROPPED me off downtown at the Muhlebach I headed for my room to go over my notes and get my questions ready for the next day. Earlier I'd made a list of who and what I wanted him to talk about and it covered eight full pages in a big legal pad. The fact that he'd sat in the front row for the Louis-Conn fight was no surprise, because every fight he'd seen at Madison Square was probably from first row center. As a matter of fact a great deal of his life had been exactly that, front row center. In his heyday he made more than five thousand dollars a week—but as he said he would go through it like a streak and wind up broke on Monday morning having to borrow money to buy gas. He'd said it all when he said, "I have trouble holding onto the old green."

One year he had forty tailored suits and thirty pairs of custom-made shoes—one pair he told me had seed pearls in the toes. For eleven months of one of his flush years, he stayed in the best hotels in the country but by December he and his first wife, Janet, wound up living in a boxcar in North Dakota. But it wasn't all bad in North Dakota, the Sioux Indians made him an honorary chieftain and later their wise men worked him into one of the Sioux myths where he heroically "bean balled" an evil Indian commissioner and saved the tribe. . . . Now how in the hell could I find that?

The celebrities who crowded around him and socialized with him included Wallace Beery, Billie Holliday, Jelly Roll Morton, Dizzy Dean, Louis Armstrong, Orson Welles, Cab Calloway, and Latin dictators Rafael Trujillo and Fulgencio Batista. He'd sung with Al Hibbler and Louis Prima; got in the ring and did quick exhibitions with Joe Louis, Sugar Ray Robinson, and John Henry Lewis; danced with Bojangles, who was also best man at his wedding to Janet; played basketball with Meadowlark Lemon and Goose Tatum of the Harlem Globetrotters; made a movie with Robert Mitchum and Julie London; and had even worked a few nights on stage in two or three of the big touring medicine shows. Not a bad résumé for a guy who at the same time was busy breaking record after record pitching while filling the stadiums with record-breaking screaming fans who loved everything he did and every move he made. No, there was no one out there like him. No, there was no one out there even close to him. And no, not from where I was sitting, would there ever be anyone quite like Leroy "Satchel" Paige.

The records show that in 1948, after Satchel had been pitching for more than twenty years in the Negro Leagues and barnstorming around the country and down into the Caribbean and South America with his famous All-Stars, he was signed to pitch for the Cleveland Indians. In one of his early starts—against the Chicago White Sox—he pitched before the strangest baseball crowd ever assembled: Comiskey Park in Chicago was jammed with Paige fans and there were more than seven thousand outside the park listening on car radios; inside the park were four to five thousand more standing in the corridors and on the steps behind the supports unable to see anything. Many said they just wanted to be near him when he pitched his first major league game in Chicago. They were there just to be there and to show their appreciation of what they were calling, and are still calling, the Chicago debut in the major leagues of the greatest pitcher, black or white, of all times. The crowds who were there and couldn't see, could only shout, whistle, and scream when they heard the news that Satch had done something. And he did do something. Something amazing. Something extraordinary.

On that night in Chicago, at age forty-two, he pitched the whole nine innings for a five to nothing shutout, allowing only five hits, and he didn't walk a single man. Ten days later, back in Cleveland, before an official crowd of 78,382 paid attendance, which is their all-time record for a night game, he shut the Sox out again. Now you talk about a debut.

The records of those games are no more extraordinary or astonishing than the records of Satchel's whole career. In many books he's credited with 250 shutouts and at least twenty-five no-hitters. He has pitched doubleheaders back to back and won both games, and it's been estimated that he appeared in more than five thousand games. His favorite showman's trick, and centerpiece, was to call in his entire infield and outfield and let them play poker on the mound behind him while he struck out the side. And when he pitched for the Chattanooga Black Lookouts and the Kansas City Monarchs at the peak of his prime, the management, who weren't in business to lose money, would post the incredible one-of-a-kind sign announcing:

WORLD'S GREATEST PITCHER LEROY "SATCHEL" PAIGE
GUARANTEED TO STRIKE OUT THE FIRST NINE MEN
OR YOUR MONEY BACK.

The teams back then—the Homestead Grays, the Chattanooga Black Lookouts, the Birmingham Black Barons, the Mobile Tigers, Gus Greenlee's Pittsburgh Crawfords, and the famous Kansas City Monarchs—were extraordinary. Almost as extraordinary as the men who played with them: Poindexter Williams, Bullet Joe Rogan, Sweet Juice Johnson, Home Run Brown, and Cool Papa Bell, who Satch said was so fast he could turn out the light and be in bed before it went out, and could get from first to second with three strides and a slide. Satch had also played with and lived with perhaps the greatest home run hitter of all time, Josiah "Josh" Gibson.

These men loved and lived baseball. They ate it, slept it, and stayed with it because that was all they knew. They knew nothing else, and if they had to, they would have probably played for nothing. When the season ended in the winter, they headed for the tropics and played for Trujillo or Batista or anyone who could fill the stands. They didn't work for quick loan operations or do dog food commercials; all they knew and all they cared about was baseball. And as Satch kept saying. "Oh, but they could play, pod-ner."

After I made my notes I stretched out on the bed, and closing my eyes I could still hear him talking. He was talking about the men and the games and the crowds and what the country was like when he was barnstorming across the South and up through the Dakotas and into Canada. And as I lay there trying to figure out how a man could be close to sixty and look around forty and move as if he were still thirty, I knew I was going to learn a lot about baseball and the Negro League and a great deal about Leroy Satchel Paige.

The press who'd made up slogans and "rules to live by" and his not eating fried foods and his Uncle Tom demeanor had trivialized him and made him more comic than heroic. And in doing so they had done Satchel Paige and all baseball, black or white, a grave injustice. And as I lay there trying to think how I was going to write about him, the one thing I knew for certain was that I was going to do something very, very different.

Before I turned the lights out I looked over the quotes I'd written down from other players and one from his mother.

"Night Train" Lane, who played football for the Detroit Lions, was named to the NFL all-star team five times, and played in six Pro Bowl games, said one day when he was playing baseball in the Negro League he found himself sitting on a curbstone crying in the rain in Council Bluffs, Iowa, because the game against Satchel Paige had been canceled. He said, "I knew I'd never get another chance to bat against him. I tell you it almost broke my heart. That's how important he was to me."

Dizzy Dean on Satch: "If me and Satch had been together at St. Louis, we would've clinched the pennant by July and gone fishing from then until it was time to come back for the World Series. He was, without any doubt, the greatest pitcher I've ever seen. And I've been looking in the mirror for a long, long time."

Bob Feller: "The prewar Paige was the best I ever saw. And I'm judging him on the way he overpowered or outwitted some of the best big league hitters of the day."

Yogi Berra: "I never knew a man who could put water that hot on his arm the way he did. That stuff would be smoking and would have scalded the average man. But Satch loved it. I hit him a few times toward the end of his career and he still had plenty of stuff on the ball. I wish I'd gotten to bat against him earlier."

Bill Veeck, when Satch was pitching for the lowly St. Louis Browns in the fifties: "I've never seen anything quite like Leroy. He's been my hero since 1934 when I saw him beat a Dizzy Dean All-Star team one to nothing in thirteen innings in California. Last year, when the wise men were saying he'd come apart if he pitched in more than three innings once a week, he worked in almost a third of all our games and won twelve and saved ten for us. He was easily the best relief man in the league, in my opinion, and the only Brownie to make the All-Star team."

Clint Courtney, his catcher with the St. Louis Browns: "You hear about pinpoint control, but Paige is the only man I've ever seen who really has it. He threw me six strikes out of ten pitches over a chewing gum wrapper one time. And his fastball still burns my mitt when he lets it go, which is whenever he needs it. Finally, he just thinks faster than most hitters. Satchel is a very smart man."

An unidentified catcher: "A good fastball will have a little hop on it at the end, then it will look like it's going to disappear. Satch has thrown balls that the batter didn't strike at and the catcher didn't catch and the umpire didn't call. Somewhere out there in the sixty feet, from the mound to the plate, they just disappeared."

Satch's mother: "All he's doing is living a shiftless, sinful life. And all I can do is keep writing and reminding him to go to Mass and be careful of gambling and the wild women out there."

Satch about his mother's problem: "I wish she'd do a turn-around on baseball. It's a terrible strain on you when your mama ain't behind you."

And finally Satch on himself: "All this coming and going. Rookies flying up the road and old-timers flying down, and nobody in between but me and old John Mize, standing pat, watching them go on by.

"And I ain't even so sure about old John. Maybe he's flying on too. If he is, I can always watch them go by myself. Time ain't going to mess with me."

I'D THOUGHT SATCH'S popularity at the Twilight Lounge and his reception at Gates's had prepared me for anything at the Flamingo, but I wasn't even close. As we entered the big club, which featured a neon flamingo behind the bandstand and a silver revolving ball over the dance floor, the band suddenly stopped playing "Precious Love" and a spotlight picked him up coming through the tables wearing a dark blue, beautifully cut suit, a red glow-in-the-dark tie, and a yellow straw boater, which looked like something tap dancers wore back in the twenties. A drum started rolling and the orchestra leader boomed out, "Ladies and Gentlemen, may I have your attention please. With us tonight is Mister Baseball himself. Here he is folks! Let's hear it for, Kansas City's favorite citizen Mis-ter Le-roy Sat-chel Paige."

Satch, turning in a circle so he could see everyone, waggled his hat and showboated across the floor waving and shouting out to his friends. When he got to the dance floor he pointed his hat at the leader. "Hey, Monroe, you keep on playing 'Precious Love.' That's one of my all-time favorites. Me and Al Hibbler knocked that thing down in Miami back in December."

Monroe grinned. "Anything you want, Satch. You letting me join your table."

Satch raked his hat on a hard angle on the side of his head

and making a pistol with his forefinger fired off a round. "Pow! Fine with me, stud. Just be sure and bring along that good-looking little singer."

The manager quickly led us to the best table on the floor, right up front in the center, and told the waiter to serve us two of the best bottles of champagne in the house. He had his hand on Satch's shoulder. "Boy, it's so good to see you. You looking great, I swear to God you are."

"You too, Derrick. You looking as sharp as ever. Hey now, I want you to meet Bo here, from Columbia, South Carolina. He's in town doing a story on me for *Holiday Magazine*. And I guarantee he's going to be saying something real nice about the Flamingo. Am I right or am I wrong, Bo?"

"Right, Satch."

Monroe and his singer, his girlfriend, Mildred, joined us as Derrick poured the champagne and asked Satch to propose a toast. With no hesitation, it was as if he'd been doing it for a living, he rose and making a 360-degree turn with his glass held high to get in the whole room, he waited for the drumroll to stop. "To Kansas City! And all the fine, fine people in it."

Derrick refilled the glasses and then personally, and with a great flourish, opened the towel-wrapped second bottle. Meanwhile Satch was waving and calling out. "Hey now, Horace, you looking good. Hey George! Hello Gertrude, I ain't seen you in a while. And Thelma, now don't you look just wonderful."

Satch was sitting in the best seat in the house and was the absolute center of attention. After another drink he winked at me and whispered. "Keep your eye on Monroe. Mildred's making eyes at me and he doesn't know what to do." He laughed, "I got him in a rundown."

But Satch was wrong. Monroe knew exactly what to do. He called the break off and dragged Mildred back up on the bandstand where they cranked up a big rhythm number that got the whole room dancing. Satch tipped his chair back, with his hands behind his head, and still wearing his yellow skimmer he was smiling up at the ceiling. He was in heaven.

At this time a tall mocha-skinned beauty, deadpan, and all by herself, came shimmying through the tables and stopped right in front of Satch. Slowly she raised her arms straight up, and still expressionless, suddenly went into a wild vibrating, jungle dance. Satch machine-gunned both hands on the table faster and faster. "It's the Dog! Got to be the Dog! Man, that's so good I can hardly stand it." When she stopped he slid a chair out for her and with a broad showman's flourish made the introductions. Her name was Lisa.

Satch let her know what I was there for and he winked at me. "Come on, Bo, hit me with some more questions for this article, you're doing."

I went along with it and asked him to tell us about getting up on stage in the southern medicine shows.

Satch, hamming it up for Lisa, sat forward grinning. "Of course you've got to realize I was only a youngster back then. Green as grass and a couple years short of shaving. But I wasn't afraid of nothing, especially anything that had to do with getting up on stage. That's something I've always loved. But yeah, hell yeah, I'd get up there with two or three of those outfits. And let me tell you something all we did was have fun. Listen to this lineup; he ticked them off on his fingers: Silas Green from New Orleans, the Great Bartok Minstrels, Rabbit Foot out of Vicksburg, and Snookum Nelson and His Creole Brothers. All that crowd were out there running around making money faster than they could count it and every one of them were as slick as greased greyhounds. Now I'm talking slick; slick shows, slick music, slick everything. And every one of them treated me and my team like we were some kind of royalty.

"Most of the time I'd sit out on the end of the minstrel line and be Mr. Bones." He was sitting in close and speaking directly to Lisa. "See, sugar foot, this is how this setup worked." He pushed the glasses aside and placed the ashtray in the center of the table and flanked it with the saltshaker on one side and the pepper on the other. He tapped the ashtray. "Now right here is where your Mister Interlocutor sat, and he is the man who runs the show."

He tapped the salt to the right. "And this is Mister Tambo, that's the guy with the tambourine. And right here," he slid the pepper over, "is Mister Bones, and that's me. I had me a set of bones and I'd do hambones and a couple of rhythms. But the main thing Tambo and me would do was make fun of Mr. Interlocutor. See he spoke like an English gentleman and old Tambo and me we'd sound like morons with harelips that didn't know nothing. But every joke we cracked we got the laughs, and every time Mr. Interlocutor opened his mouth he got the boos."

Lisa was laughing and Satch was spreading it on thick. "Now these jokes weren't much. Matter of fact they were pretty lousy by today's standards but when you got that chorus line going and those costumes and that wild music, everything you do gets funny. Like old Mister Interlocutor would start off by saying, 'Mis-ter Bones.' And he'd pronounce it just so. And I'd say, 'Yes-sir Mis-ter Inter-locutor.' And right away you'd know I was making fun of him. And right away that crowd was on my side laughing at him. Ain't nothing a bunch of plow jockeys and rednecks like better than to have someone like Mr. Bones making fun of someone like Mr. Interlocutor.

"Anyhow, he'd say, 'Mis-ter Bones, who was that lady I saw you with last night?'

"And I'd roll my eyes and cock my head over and act like I didn't hear him. 'What was that you said, Mis-ter Interlocutor?'

"See, sugar foot, now he's got to ask me again. And right in here the audience is falling down it's gotten so funny. I mean it, it was wild. Anyhow he'd say it again. 'Mis-ter Bones, I merely asked you who was that lady I saw you with last night?'

"And I'd waggle my head and roll my eyes some more and elbow whoever was sitting next to me and say. 'Why Mis-ter In-ter-locutor, that was no lady. That was your wife.'

"And that crowd would be laughing so hard they'd fall right out of their chairs." He turned to me. "Bo, remind me to tell you about them chairs." Then back to Lisa. "And then, sugar foot, right then the band would strike up with something like

'Sweet Georgia Brown' and me and Tambo would whip out to the front of the stage whirl around and do a little dance. Now it wasn't much, just a time step with a little Charleston thrown in. But then we'd go into our big cakewalk. Now that was our number one main move."

Satch raised a hand. "Hold it. Hold the phone right here. Because the cakewalk is something that you cannot explain. That's something you got to see."

And with that Satch was on his feet waving to Monroe on the bandstand. "Professor, let's have a little 'Georgia Brown.' And let me hear plenty of that bass underneath and up front. I've got to show this gal a little something."

Monroe sang out, "You got it, Satch."

The music came up with plenty of bass, and Satch, with his hat almost covering his eyes and his elbows up and out in an exaggerated akimbo and the spotlight tracking his every move, cakewalked to the big and raucous beat all the way across the room. Lisa, and everyone in the room, was standing up and on the chairs so they could see better, clapping, cheering, and whistling as he crossed the floor, made a big, arm-spread circus turn and came back. Then holding his hat high and pointing it up at the silver ball he did a double spin, followed it with a quick bow, and sat back down still in the spotlight. What a showman!

About this time Lisa's boyfriend showed up and took her back to her table but not until after she'd whispered a number of things in Satch's ear. As she was leaving he motioned for Mildred, who was up on the bandstand, to come join us just as Derrick and his headwaiter arrived with an oversize platter of bite-size sandwiches, forty or fifty miniature hot dogs wrapped in bacon, and two more bottles of champagne. Just another quiet night at the Flamingo.

"IS THAT SATCHEL Paige you're with? I heard he was in Hollywood making another movie. Or living someplace down in South America."

I was in the bathroom and a distinguished man in a three-piece suit cornered me at the sink. "No, that's him all right. He's looking good too isn't he?"

Suddenly he opened his vest and shirt, whipped up his undershirt, and stuck out his chest. "Take a look. Take a look. Solid gray not a black hair in there. You find a black hair and I'll eat it."

Counting this guy's black hairs wasn't what I had in mind, so I finished drying my hands and started for the door. He grabbed my arm. "Hold it mister. I'm straight, I swear I am. I got two kids and another one on the way. You got to hear this. I played ball with Satch over twenty years ago, right here in Kansas City. Hell's bells, we were on the road together; we were all over the South. And look at him; he ain't got a single gray hair on him. What I want to know is how in the hell he does it? I'm saying maybe that ain't Satch."

"It's Satch all right." I told him I was doing a story on him and asked him to join us.

At first Satch didn't remember him, but he faked it and said he did to make him feel good. Then he did, and they began talking about the Kansas City Monarchs back in the forties and fifties. The man was Charley Davis and he'd played two years in the Negro League and one with the Monarchs' traveling team before he quit and went into the concrete business. He ordered another bottle for the table and I raised the ante and bought two more. This was going to be a very good night.

Charley said, "Satch, I caught for you a five or six times and remember it like it was yesterday. You'd practice over a damn Wrigley's Juicy Fruit gum wrapper instead of home plate. Hell, one time you said you were too sharp for the wrapper and I had to put a dime on it for a target." He cut his eyes at me. "I'll put my hand on a Bible on that one. Ain't I right, Satch?"

Satch nodded. "You're right, Charley. Dead level right. I had my control going. Like the man said, I could thread a needle in the night." He winked at me. "Bo, when we get out to the house, I'll show you the old posters we used to put up. Charley, tell this cracker what we were advertising back then and what we said we'd do. I already told him once but I don't think he believed me."

Charley spread his hands wide. "They were about four feet wide and, let's see, about so high." He held his hand at eye level. "And they said, 'Kansas City Monarchs present Leroy Satchel Paige, world's greatest pitcher. Guaranteed to strike out the first nine men or your money back.' Is that right, Satch?"

"Damn straight."

The waitress filled our glasses and Charley pointed his up at the revolving ball tracking tiny colored lights around the room and up across the ceiling. "Those were good times, Satch. I swear they were. Lord once in a while, like right now, I'd give anything to be back there."

Satch studied the silver ball over the rim of his glass. "Yeah they were Charley. They won't be seeing times like that anymore. Not around here they won't. . . . And you didn't have to spend a damn fortune to enjoy them. Everything cost a nickel there for a long time; hot dogs a nickel, candy a nickel, peanuts a nickel. Hell, it only cost a dime to get in and if you had a car you could park it for nothing."

Satch and Charley began talking about Josh Gibson. Satch turned to me. "You got to understand, Josh was strong. He didn't have much strength from his legs—he had it all across in here." He drew a line across his chest. "But he was powerful right in through here. He hit a ball in Comiskey Park that went clean over that center field wall. They figured it had to have been over six hundred feet. Now ain't nobody ever done that. Probably never will.

"Bo, if I was a writer I could write a book about Josh just by himself. See, he was my catcher all those years we were playing with the Monarchs and the Crawfords. Plus all that time we put in barnstorming around the country and down in Cuba and Mexico and South America with my All-Stars. Me and Josh were just like that." He held up two fingers side by side. "We roomed together, played together, chased women together. And every once in a while we'd catch us one of them. Hell, I'm telling you something here, we did everything together.

"Josh caught for me on my All-Star team when we beat Dizzy Dean's All-Stars and then when we beat Bob Feller's. And those were number one teams. Number one. See Dizzy's team was all from the National League. But Bob Rapid's—that's what I called him, Bob Rapid—was from the best of both leagues, the National and the American. I got all this stuff out at the house, photographs, the batting orders, the clippings, everything, you'll see it when we get out there. But you talk about some first-class teams, those were sure as hell two of them right there. When that series was over, I mean between my All-Stars and Dizzy's and then Bob Feller's, we'd won six games and they'd won four. Bo, we not only could play with anyone, we could beat them like a drum almost every time we felt like it. Ain't that right, Charley?"

Charley was smiling so hard he was crying. He had to go for a napkin. "We sure could, Satch. We sure as hell could."

Satch was still thinking about Josh Gibson. "For my money

I'd say he was the strongest home run hitter the game ever knew. It was terrible he had to go and die so damn young like that. Picked up a cancer or something and it was terrible.

"What me and Josh did there for a while was we'd pick up a good glove man for third base and we'd travel around in my station wagon putting on exhibitions. We played all around in here, up in Canada, and all down South. See, we'd recruit six local boys from the town we were in for our team and we'd play anybody. Anybody, anywhere, anytime. See, the folks would come out to see me pitch and Josh hit and they would pack those stands. It didn't matter who we had in the infield and outfield. When you see my posters you'll see how it says

WORLD'S GREATEST HOME RUN HITTER
JOSH GIBSON. GUARANTEED TO HIT
THREE HOME RUNS OR YOUR MONEY BACK.

"And let me tell you something I bet we never gave one penny of that money back."

Later, after the Flamingo closed, Satch, Charley, Derrick, the club owner, and I were still at our table, still talking baseball. Everyone had gotten tired of champagne and we were tapering off on beer. Derrick, who'd actually been to Satch's debut game in Chicago back in '48, said he'd paid a hundred dollars for the ticket. "Hell, I'd have paid five hundred. Lot of boys did, I'm not kidding. That was the most important game in my life." He cupped his hand over Satch's shoulder. "How bout it, old boy, what was it like out there on that mound? I mean that first minute you stepped out there."

It was the same dumb question I'd asked him back in the Twilight Zone Lounge. But this time he just made a couple of moisture rings with the bottom of his bottle as he thought about it. "I'll tell you this much, it was nice. Yeah, that's what it was, nice. Real nice." He made another ring with his bottle. "And I'll tell you something else. I wouldn't mind being around them boys again. I still got my Stinger going and I can still hold any team breathing three or four innings. Charley boy, you wait a few more days. All I need is some muffler work on my wagon and I'm going to be busting out of here. I got my All-Stars all ready and they're raring to go. If I'm lying, I'm dying."

Satch got up and went over to the jukebox and came back whistling. "I can't stand it too long without any music. Derrick, you got you some nice Johnny Mercer songs on that machine. Now there's the boy that could write the tunes. I love his stuff. I met him once in L.A., fine boy, fine. Hell, Bo, he's from Savannah, Georgia, down in your neck of the woods. Hey I'll tell you who else is from down in there; Larry Doby who is one first-rate ballplayer."

Derrick asked, "What all did this Mercer guy write?"

Satch acted like he couldn't believe he'd asked the question. "Lord, Derrick, you ought to know that. What did he write? It was more like what all didn't he write. He wrote a hundred tunes and every one of them is number one, top notch. Top notch. Listen to this," he began ticking them off on his fingers. "'Candy,' 'Lazy Bones.' He wrote that with Hoagy Carmichael. 'Accentuate the Positive,' 'Georgia on My Mind,' 'Moon River,' 'The G.I. Jive,' 'Tangerine,' 'Laura.' Hell, he even wrote 'Zippity-Doo-Dah.' Now I'll tell you my all-time top of the line favorite, 'Skylark.' That is one fine tune. I could listen to that thing ten times in a row and never get tired of it. Hey, and here's another one, 'Summer Wind.' Now that ain't too bad a tune either."

Satch wanted to talk about music, and I took over the table and told them how my dad had a five-piece radio group of two whites and three blacks back in Columbia who called themselves "the Hawaiians," and how they claimed they were just in from Waikiki Beach in Honolulu. Then they'd play the only song they knew in Hawaiian, "My Little Grass Shack in Kealakekua, Hawaii." After Kealakekua, every song was Spanish. I told them that Dad said no one in Richland County would know the difference. But someone did and they called in and Dad and his group were out of work and back on the street.

Satch waited until I wound down, then he said, "I pitched in

Honolulu a few years back and we went over to see Don Ho. Now there's a boy that puts on a show. Hell, that old boy found out I was in the crowd and put the light on me and dragged me up to sit with him at the piano. We joked around a little and then we cracked down on 'Tiny Bubbles.' Y'all remember that one? That's his theme song.

"Now we're talking music." Satch's eyes were shining and he leaned forward dying to tell us something. "Listen here, let me tell y'all who I had a few drinks and spent a little time with down in New Orleans. Now this wasn't exactly yesterday. Hold it, tell you what I'm going to do. I'm going to make you guess who it was. Come on, take a crack at it."

Derrick said, "Billie Holliday."

Satch said, "No it wasn't Billie. But we're real good friends too. Now there's a gal I dearly love. No, this was way on back."

Charley said, "Louis Armstrong?"

"No, but we were buddies too. That fool loved his red beans and rice. Loved baseball too. Hell, what you talking about, he had his own team. The New Orleans Armstrongs. But this is back before Louis's time. No, now I'm going to take that one back, it was right at the same time as Louis."

I said, "Fletcher Henderson." He shook his head again.

We rattled off Bunny Berigan, Louis Prima, and finally Bessie Smith. It turned out he knew them all and that Bessie Smith had a sister, "Walking Mary" Smith, who was a great blues singer in the Rabbit Foot Minstrels, one of the shows Satch had been in.

We named a few more and he kept shaking his head, "Y'all ain't even close. You got to go back further. Way on back. OK, here it is, you'll never get him. You ready? Mister Jelly Roll Morton. His real name is Frederick La Menthe. I met up with him when he was playing the clubs in the French Quarter. See, this was back when I was pitching for Chattanooga, that was the first big team I was on. Well anyway, we had a few drinks together. That crazy fool was drinking that absinthe mess."

He shuddered, "Stuff will give you the vertigo and the

tremens and drive your ass to the rack. Anyhow, we were yakking away about this kind of music and that kind of music. You know that old fool said he invented jazz. And you know something, if you listen to him play and hear all the songs that scutter wrote you got to damn well believe him. But that night he didn't want to talk too much music, he wanted to talk about clothes. I never believed it but I heard when he died he had over a thousand suits.

"Anyhow, he tells me, 'Youngblood'—now you know this has got to be back there if some bird is calling me youngblood. Anyhow, he said, 'you come with me and I'll show you one or two sharp outfits.'

"OK, so now I'm saying to myself, I'm saying, Satch, this guy's a straight up fairy and he's going to get you up in his room and there's no telling what kind of tricks he's going to try and pull. Hell, he might even have a gun.

"Then I says to myself, But man, this bird's too thin and worn down to do too much damage. So I said, 'Come on Mr. Jelly Roll let me see them suits. Ain't nothing I like better than fine clothes.'

"So we went up to his rooms, I think he was living on Rampart Street or someplace pretty close."

Satch had the table's attention and he was milking it. "Lord, I thought I had some clothes and some shoes but when he started laying out suits and shirts and shoes on his bed, I like to fell out. I've never seen stuff like that before or since, it was like a rainbow had come in that room. He had him an orange suit and a purple suit and a damn yellow one. I mean it, yellow. Yellow as a lemon with yellow shoes and socks and suspenders to go with it.

"And that crazy fool had women lined up four deep that wanted to go out with him just so they could be seen with him. They'd do anything he wanted them to do as long as he let them hang around. See, you got to realize, there wasn't a helluva lot of money in music back then so a lot of those boys hustled pool and hustled the women and did all kinds of jobs. Hell, what you talking about, a lot of them worked for the city cleaning the streets and picking up garbage. Now ain't that a bitch? Playing that beautiful music all night and then getting up in the morning to go out and pick up garbage?

"Anyhow, Jelly Roll had all the moves, I mean all of them: piano, pool, dice, clothes, and women. He always said most men got women figured out all wrong. They think what you need to get a women is money and cars and furs and jewels. But that ain't it at all. He said the way to get women is to have other women crowding in around you. That way the others want to see what they missing and they'll join right in. But see, along with all this high living and the women, old Jelly Roll was a number one musician and a number one composer. He was raised a Creole and he knew music inside and out. I mean classical music: operas, symphonies, and beautiful Creole lullabies. I'm telling you, you could name a tune, any tune, and that boy would just reach over and play it for you. It was a pleasure being with him.

"Most musicians can't read note one but Jelly Roll could do it, read it, play it, and write it. I swear to God once he got to talking you figured that man knew everything. He told me he'd write his music so complicated, with so many twists and turns and change of keys, no one could steal it because no one could play it but him. And I believe him. Tell you what he wrote. He wrote 'Muskrat Ramble' and 'Wolverine Blues,' and hey catch this, he wrote 'Tiger Rag.' Hey now, I'm betting the table ten dollars none of you know what 'hold that tiger' means."

Derrick said, "Just what it says. When you get a hold of a tiger you better hold on or he'll nail your ass."

"Nope, ain't even close. How about you, Bo?"

"I'm with Derrick. I thought the same thing."

Satch tipped his glass and poured his beer. "A tiger is the lowest hand you can have in poker. So when you want to bluff and bluff big you got to hold that tiger. Nine out of ten people you talk to nowadays don't know what in the hell you're talking about. But if you down in the Quarter they'll tell you right off the bat. I'll tell you what else that fool did, he invented 'stride piano,' that's when that left hand is going up and down so fast you can barely see it. Hell, he's got a tune called 'Finger-buster' that no one could play but him. That's how good he was. But I don't know about him inventing jazz; he had to be lying on that one because that stuff goes way on back."

Derrick signaled for another round and asked Satch to talk some more about Jelly Roll. Satch said, "No man, it's getting late, I just can't be coming in any later than this. Lahoma is going to crawl all over my butt."

Charley said, "Dammit Satch, you can't leave us like this."

I said, "Yeah come on. I can use all this stuff."

Satch reconsidered, then he looked around the room to make sure no one could hear him but us. Then he rocked forward on his elbows and touched the tips of his fingers together, very lightly. "Tell you what I'm going to do for you boys, I'm going to pretend I'm Jelly Roll. I know exactly how that old fool sounded. Now listen close. First off he called himself the suit man from suit land."

Satch repeated, "the suit man from suit land" and the line rose and fell; it was the calypso hop and Creole mix he wanted. "There that's it, the suit man from suit land. See, Jelly had that Creole French Quarter accent and he was one educated son of a bitch. See how he'd cut his words off like I'm doing? See, he'd be pronouncing every word real careful and real precise. It had to be just so, or he wouldn't have it. Everything has to be just so. And that's the way he wrote and that's the way he played his music and worked his women and that's the way he wore his suits. I'm telling you, all that man wore was suits. I swear I never saw him in anything but a suit and a white shirt or a colored stripe and a good looking silk necktie." He paused and went on. "OK, here he goes now. I'm going to do him talking."

Satch's voice went higher and smoother, picking up a soft, sliding elegance as he stretched everything out, way out. "I'd come into a town like Mobile, Alabama, or Greenville, Missis-sippi, or say Bi-lox-i, Miss-iss-ip-pi, and I'd get me a room right down there in the middle of town. First thing I'd do was I'd put on a sharp wide pinstripe and some fine shoes with pearl button spats and a homburg and I'd go stand on the corner for about ten or fifteen minutes smoking a French cigarette, the blue kind, in a long bone holder with maybe a little gold and silver trim. And I'd just stand there looking like I was supposed to be meeting someone. Someone very important. Then after a while I'd go back to my room and change into something sharper, something like an orange suit."

Satch gave orange two full beats, or-ange. "And I'd put on a pair of high-powered black-and-white checked Chicago flats and a straw skimmer hat with a black and orange silk band running around it. See, the orange in that band would pick up on the orange in the suit. And that was a very nice touch. Then I'd go back out to that same spot and take a nice long look at my fingernails."

Satch rolled his long fingers over in a slow articulated flourish, demonstrating. "Say about like this."

Charley, Derrick, and I were laughing so hard we were crying.

Satch took a long drag on his cigarette and held it out studying the ash. "Then after another fifteen or twenty minutes I'd go back and change into something extraordinary. Something like a purple suit with white trim and a purple skimmer and purple shoes. See everything purple, including the socks. Especially the socks. And man you got to be knowing, that would cold solid get the attention. Because the next thing you know some fine-looking frail would come sidling up and say, 'Mister, you sure have you a lot of fine-looking suits.'

"And I'd say, 'Baby doll, I could change suits like this all day every day for a whole week and still have several left over to go to church on Sunday. Several, baby doll, several; I am the suit man from suit land.'"

Satch slapped his hand flat on the table. "That's what that fool called himself, the suit man from suit land. Then he'd say, 'The next thing you knew that girl would be with me up in my room and I'd be treating her real nice. Then I'd take her out and buy her a couple nice silk dresses and a couple big hats that I would personally pick out. And I'd get a photographer to take a nice picture of us together. One for me and one for her.'

"'Yessir, everything would be working out fine because about two or three days after this she'd be out on the street working for me. In the meantime I'd find me a good pool hall where I could hustle some eight- or nine-ball and a good cathouse where I could play piano. . . . Yessiree Bi-lox-i. Biloxi, Mississippi, right down there on the tip, was one fine, fine, fine, town.'"

Charley looped his arm around Satch's shoulders. "Man, that is one terrific story. I don't know when I enjoyed myself so much."

Satch said, "Same here old buddy. You know the more I look at you the more I remember a lotta things about you. You always kept your thumbs up like this," he hitchhiked them up, "when you were jangling around trying to get loose. Hell, I nicknamed you 'Thumbs.' You sure as hell got to remember that."

Charley flipped his thumbs up, cocked his head, and clicked his tongue. "I'll be damned. Well how about that."

Satch was smiling, "And when you squatted down behind that plate you'd cup your right hand over your balls up real high." He soft-punched him on the shoulder. "Hope you're still doing that? Take a lick down there and it's all over."

Charley shook a cigarette out. "Satch, this is the greatest night for me in a long time. This is just like it was back when we were playing."

Satch flipped open a book of matches with one hand and in the same smooth one-handed motion, and with some nifty finger work, lit it. Then leaning in close he looped his arm around Charley's shoulders. "Charley boy, tell you what you got to do. Come out to the park tomorrow and watch me warming up. Maybe me and you can start doing some talking."

"About what, Satch?"

"About you watching me throw a few and checking out how I still got my stuff going."

"And then what?"

"Then maybe we make us some plans about you coming with me when I bust out of here and go on the road. I'm talking about another barnstorming tour. Just me and you and an infield. I got me some kids all lined up that can field and hit but right now I need me a catcher. Now listen, I'll tell my agent to book us a few games. Hell, we can get all the games we can handle."

Charley was listening, but he wasn't buying. "Just six of us. How's that work?"

"Simple. That's all we need. The team we're playing loans us outfielders or anyone else we need. They'll kill to play with us. I mean it. See all those fans still want to see if I can still throw it. Hell, a lot of them will pay good money just to see that I'm still standing up and kicking."

Charley's voice dropped, "Sounds fine to me." But I could tell he didn't mean it.

Satch squeezed Charley's shoulder. "You don't have to say yes or no right here and now. All I want you to do is come out to the park tomorrow and you see what you see and then you tell me what you want to do. But I'm telling you something here, Charley, we could solid have us some times. And we can pick up some pretty good money. All I got to do is get my muffler fixed. I got that damn thing wired up with a coat hanger, and I'm not about to go down the road with that thing dragging and throwing sparks. There ain't nothing any sorrier looking than that."

Charley excused himself and went to the men's room. Satch snapped his fingers. "Goddamn me and my motor mouth. He was all ready to go there for a while and I crowded him too close. Dammit, I just don't know when to shut up."

I knew he hadn't been out in over three years but I had to ask the question. "You really going to go barnstorming again?"

He flared up, "Damn right I'm going barnstorming again. I

went last year and I went the year before that. And the year before that. Why in the hell can't I go again?"

"Just asking."

Charley came back. As he was sitting down Satch said, "Charley boy, let's forget tomorrow I got too much I got to do. That make you feel better?"

Charley said, "I don't feel bad, Satch, I swear I don't. I just thought, hell I'm fifty-six years of age. Both of us are getting on up there. And that living on the road can get a little rough."

"OK, just put it out of your mind. Maybe you're right. Maybe I ought to take a year off and just rest up. But tell you what you can do for me. You come out to the Twilight tomorrow around four and we'll kick some more of this old bullshit around and see if we can give Bo here a good story. You up for that?"

Charley said, "I'll be there. But right now, Satch, how about telling me a little bit more about Jelly Roll."

"Not now, Charley. Maybe some other time."

But Charley wouldn't let up. "Well how about some of those other guys you knew down in New Orleans. The piano players and the horn men and some of those blues players. Come on, Satch, I collect this stuff. I eat it up."

I was nodding. "Yeah, come on, Satch. Same here."

Satch gave in and cocked his hat low almost over his eyes and leaned forward on his elbows. He was a natural-born storyteller. "OK, damn if y'all won't wear a man down. It was like this, old Jelly Roll loved the women but he loved the young chicks best. And like I said he could get them too. Now this is one funny-ass line, and if I wasn't so happily married I'd have stolen it way the hell on back. But this one belongs to Jelly. And here's exactly how he said it."

Satch went into his high and overarticulated Creole delivery. "Gentlemen, if you ever see Mister Jelly Roll Morton in the company of an older woman you will know one of two things. One, I am in her custody and we're on our way to jail. Or two, she is taking me to a much younger girl." He laughed, slapped the table, and had to say it again. "'Taking me to a much younger girl.' Man, that's exactly what that old son of a bitch said."

Charley was laughing and shaking his head. "Dammit, now that was too short. Satch that don't even count. Come on man, loosen up."

Satch was loving all this. "Well, OK, one more. One more. Now this is the last one. The last one, then I got to go. OK, see, there was this big old coal black trombone player, hell I forget his name now, he must have weighed three hundred. This guy was huge. Had to sit on two seats he was so wide. Know what I mean? Anyhow, he played in the band with Jelly Roll. Jelly always had his own band. He liked to say 'Gentlemen, I've had several very large bands in my time, several. And I intend having several more before I run my string out.'" He rocked his head, "That boy loved to say 'several.'"

"Anyhow, one night this big old buck had him a little high yellow gal in one of the booths at this joint where we were shooting nine-ball and I heard them yakking away. See, this guy was so big all he had to do was clear his throat and you could hear him across the damn street.

"Anyhow, this little gal said, 'Chauncey.' Hey that's his name. I knew it would come back. Yeah that's it, Chauncey, Chauncey Dubose. That scutter played trombone and trumpet. Jelly was always bitching how he couldn't read note one. But man that fool could lift the ceiling right off the room with his power. He was stronger than Louis Armstrong and that's saying something. Anyhow, this little high yellow gal wasn't any bigger than a piece of soap and she had this high-pitched screech voice that would make your damn ears ring.

"So there they were, old Chauncey, who sounded like he was talking out of a goddamn coal mine, and this little heifer who was snip snipping away high enough to break the brandy glasses, and they were trying to negotiate the evening. Yeah, that's what they were trying to do, negotiate the evening. Know what I mean? Now they were trying to keep their voices down, see, they didn't want everybody hearing their business. But it wasn't no use because every word they said was every word we heard. I mean now this was one funny-ass scene. So this little heifer squeezes out something like"—Satch's voice went thin and up into a high falsetto—"'Chauncey, I got to go home now.' Then she puffs up, you know how they do, and she huffs, 'My momma is sitting up waiting for me right this minute, and, she will not go to bed until I get there.'

"Well old Chauncey makes one of those deep alligator rumbles in the bottom of his lungs and says, 'Sugar, you ain't going nowhere. You done sat there and drank up all my beer money. Now you telling me you're going home alone. No ma'am, you are not going home alone. You know what me and you are going to do?'

"And now right in here this little gal is really getting mad. And the madder she gets the more she's biting everything off like it's coming through a bunch of razor blades. She says, 'Well Mister Big Spender, Big Time Shot, why don't you tell me exactly what you think we're going to be doing.'

"So old Chauncey drops down a couple more floors and says. 'Baby, me and you are going to go out and we're going to ride around a little bit.'" Satch held up his hand. "Now listen what he's doing here. You talk about some nuance. This is nuance. He gets most of that line down pretty low but when he gets to, 'ride around a little bit,' that scutter drops each word lower than the last one. Like he's on some cellar steps or going down some old coal mine or something. *Ride around a little bit.* Man that line was so low and so deep and so goddamn scary you just knew if that gal got home Monday morning the first thing she's going to do is drop to her knees and thank the Lord she's still alive."

Charley was wiping his eyes with a napkin and blowing his nose. "Satch, I don't know when I've laughed so much."

Satch punched him on his shoulder. "And I don't know when I've talked so damn much. I'm running off at the mouth like a damn parrot. If somebody don't put a hood on me I'll never shut up." He snapped his fingers. "Now you be sure and come out to the Zone tomorrow. Maybe we'll talk some more."

"I'll be there. I swear I will. And hey, I ain't said no to going out on the road with you. Let me get that straight. I just want a little time to think about it. That's all, I just want to think about it."

"I gotcha, old man."

After Charley said goodnight and left, Satch finished his beer and raised his hand for the last one of the night. "Charley ain't going nowhere with me. You couldn't drag that guy out of Kansas City with a goddamn John Deere tractor."

CHAPTER 6

BUT SATCH WAS wrong. The next day at four o'clock sharp, Charley came bouncing into the Twilight Zone Lounge popping his hands and snapping his fingers. "I thought about it and thought about it." He stuck out his hand. "Satch, old buddy, old buddy, I'm with you. I'm ready to roll. All you got to do is say when and get me a uniform. I even got my mitt ready."

They shook. "That's terrific, Charley. I swear it is. I got the uniforms, plenty of them. All I got to do is get my muffler fixed, then I'm calling the agent." He hitchhiked his thumb at me. "We're getting ready to go out to the muffler shop right this second. Ain't that right, Bo?"

This was the first I'd heard about this. "Sure. Anytime you're ready."

Satch twirled his finger in the air for three beers and sat back, lighting a cigarette. "Charley, you're going to have the time of your life out there. I swear you are. There ain't nothing like it."

Charley said, "Where we going first?"

Satch exhaled and spoke through the smoke, "Hell, I forgot the name of the town; it's just the other side of Topeka. I got it written down on a piece of paper. Then we head on into Denver. We want to get there at night so we can get used to that altitude. It's about a mile higher than we are here, so I'll be putting some extra stuff on my Stinger. Charley, you're going to have to get down on your knees for it, because it's going to knock you right on your butt."

He raised up and called out to the bartender. "Rudolph, how about dialing a number for me?"

"Sure thing, Satch."

It was printed on the back of his hand. "Here you go, 243779. You got it?"

"I got it. Hey, Satch, someone called from there a while ago and left that same number."

Satch said, "Well how about that?"

Charley asked, "Is that the muffler shop?"

Satch winked at me. "Yeah, something like that."

The call went through and Satch took it at the bar. I knew it was Lisa, the girl he met at the Flamingo.

When Satch came back, Charley said, "Man, no muffler shop is going to be calling you here like that. Come on, is that the agent? What's up?"

Satch rested his hand on Charley's shoulder. "Charley boy, let's get something straight right up front here. Who I call and when I call them is my business. OK? I can't be showing you all my moves."

Charley was talking to his beer. "Well I just figured you're not going to go running around with no muffler shop printed on your hand."

"That's fine, Charley. So what we're going to do right now is leave it right there. That OK with you?"

"Yeah, Satch. OK with me."

Later when Charley left to go to the bathroom Satch asked, "Did that bird pick up any of that tab last night? I sort of lost track."

"Sure he bought a couple rounds. Maybe more."

"Good, I don't want to hook up with some creep who's going to stiff us."

"I wouldn't worry about that. Hell, he paid for most of that champagne."

"That's good. That's very good."

When Charley came back Satch told him we were going over to the muffler shop and we would meet him out at the park between six and six thirty. "Now be sure and bring your mitt. I've got some grease for it if you need it. And when you get home do you a couple stretching exercises and loosen up. You look pretty limber; you don't need too much."

Charley said, "I been working out with my kid. That boy keeps me and that old mitt in shape."

"Bring him along, he can shag balls for us."

Charley said, "Great, he'll love that."

◆

At the muffler shop a mechanic with his name, Cecil, stitched on his coveralls pocket raised the wagon up on the lift and began his inspection. He tapped the muffler, the pipes running to the manifold, and finally the pipe back out to the tail. He came out shaking his head. "You're lucky you got this far. It's all shot, every damn foot. Satch, you need it all."

Satch picked up a pair of long-handled pliers and a ball-peen hammer. "Mind if I take a look?"

"Go right ahead. But be careful, those pipes are red-hot."

Satch stooped down and went under and hollered out. "Don't worry, Bo, I've done this enough, I know what I'm doing here." He began up front and tapped his way down the pipes to the muffler and out to the tail pipe. Then he came out dusting grease chips from his hair and wiping his hands on a rag. "Cecil, I'll tell you what you do. I want you to replace that first two feet from the back of the muffler clamp and I want a new tail pipe. I can live with everything else. I'll catch it next time. That OK with you?"

"Whatever you say, Satch. It's your car."

Satch's voice was very flat, very cold. "Cecil, you are right about that."

While Cecil was unclamping the pipes Satch took me over to the Coke machine and slid in a quarter. He opened the bottle, handed it to me, and slid in another quarter. He kept his voice low but I could tell he was still mad. "Good thing I didn't leave the wagon here. You turn your back on that son of a bitch and he'll replace the whole damn engine."

It was later, after we left the muffler shop and we were on our way over to City Park, when I asked him how he paid the players he took along.

"Pretty good. Yeah, I pay them pretty good. Ten bucks a day for meals and I take care of everything else. Then when we play I take out all my car and food expenses and we split everything right across the board."

We had plenty of time to get to the park but we were going sixty in a thirty-five-mile zone. Later I found out he got caught speeding almost once a month; his insurance premiums were sky-high.

I asked, "But where do these kids come from?"

"I got a buddy who coaches American Legion ball—so most of them are kids sixteen and seventeen. They'll play all day every day and the heat doesn't give them a lick of trouble. I try to keep them young like that, that way I keep away from the winos and the pill heads. Hell, you turn your back on these drunks nowadays and they'll drink your damn shaving lotion."

CHAPTER  7

WHEN WE PULLED into the park, Charley and his son Clete were already out on the diamond tossing a ball back and forth. Satch parked, and as he slid his big canvas bag of equipment out of the back of the wagon Clete came trotting over to help. Satch told him to carry it out to the batter's box and he began walking around in a circle stretching his arms up and around his back and making long reaches straight up at the sky.

Charley was next to me. "I guess he's slowing down. Use to just light a cigarette and say 'OK I'm ready. Let me have some batters.'" He called out to Satch, "Ain't that right Satch?"

Ain't what right, Charley?"

"You used to light a cigarette and say that's all you needed to warm up."

"Right, Charley. That's exactly what I'd say. Hey, you be sure and tell Bo anything you remember like. OK?"

"OK, Satch."

Satch began lobbing soft balls in to Charley who crouched behind home plate with me standing in behind waiting to see if he had any stuff left. There was nothing on the balls but they were like long clotheslines, waist high and right over the center. Charley, staying in his squat position, cranked them back like a machine and I could tell Satch was pleased with him.

Charley hollered, "You want Clete to hit a few?"

"Naw, let me keep doing this." Satch threw two more. "OK let him stand in there. But don't be swinging at anything. I don't want to be making any sudden moves."

Clete stood in the box taking practice swings. Charley said, "OK now put it on your shoulder and keep it there. You can hit him later." After a few more pitches Charley looked back over his shoulder at me. "Watch this close. He's got it going now. The son of a gun is still warming up but watch where that ball's traveling. I haven't moved the mitt a damn inch."

He called out, "Satch, let's see a few on the outside corner."

The next ball came in knee-high and nipped the outside corner. The second followed the first, the third followed the second. So did the fourth. Four perfect pitches low and outside it was as if he'd thrown one and traced the three others over it. Charley, crouching down waiting for the fifth, looked up at me shaking his head. "This is so goddamn unbelievable. No one can do this. The son of a bitch hasn't changed a bit."

I said, "And he's throwing so easy. There's no effort there at all."

"He's always done that. But you hear that thing pop? My hand's burning up. He's got plenty speed."

"But can he do that on the road?"

Charley tossed the ball back to Satch. "From what I'm looking at right now that bastard can do anything he wants." He turned around so he could see me. "You know what? If we get out of here, we're going to have one helluva time out there."

I asked him how much his pitching had changed since he saw him last.

Charley said, "From sixty feet, I'd say not one bit. Not even one little bit. Christ, he's like Peter Pan."

I said, "That's him Peter Pan, a tall Peter Pan. I'll say one thing for him, he sure has a lot of friends. Everyone knows him."

Another ball whistled in on the outside corner, right where the last one had been. It was seven in a row, Charley whipped it back. "Yeah he does, but you know something, he never really got too close to anyone. Hard to believe but he was always a loner."

"You're kidding. Why was that?"

The ball came in again and Charley snapped it back. "I guess he was just too good at everything. Good at pitching, talking, dancing, raising hell. You name it, he was on top of it. And the women swarmed all over him, that made us all jealous. Plus he had all that money. Hell he even had his own airplanes. Two or three of them. I'm telling you, this guy was a powerful force."

The ball came in and Charley tossed it back out. "I guess you could say he was everybody's friend and at the same time he never got too close to anyone. That make any sense?"

"All the sense in the world."

He stood up from his crouch and hollered out. "That's enough for me, right now."

Satch came in from the mound. "Boy, you looked pretty good in there. How's the legs?"

A beat-up old Chevrolet pulled into the parking area and Satch's five American Legion players, still in their uniforms, climbed out and came across the outfield. Satch met them out at first base, brought them in and introduced them around. Clete knew two of them from high school, and in a few minutes they were all out on the field whipping the ball around. Clete stood in the batter's box tapping out grounders to third, to short, to second, and to first. Then he'd reverse it and go from first to second to short and then to third.

The kids looked fast and sharp but Satch kept popping his hands together and hollering. "Nathan, I want to see you getting in behind that ball. . . . Behind it. . . . Don't give me any of that off to the side crap. . . . Let's see you snap off those throws. . . . Eric, keep your butt low. Low, that's it, low. . . . OK, Bobby, good throw, now let's see you speed it up. Let's have a little pepper. . . . Let's hear a little chatter. . . . Now you're talking. . . . Now you're talking. . . . Now I'm hearing something. . . . Now you're cooking and looking like ballplayers."

Charley said, "Look at them. There's not a one of them that wouldn't die for him."

I said, "So would Clete."

"You can say that again."

It was the first time I'd gotten Charley alone and the first time I'd gotten a chance to ask him how much Satch had changed in twenty years. Charley kept watching him working out with the kids. "None when he's out on the field. Not a bit. And none up close either, he's still the same old liar. Just between me and you, they never called me Thumbs. Hell, I'd be a fool to run around like that. You fall down and you poke out your damn eyes. But see, that's the way he is. He made all that up. He's always been like that. I guess that's how he remembers everything. But see, you got to go along with it. I mean how in the hell you going to say, that ain't so, Satch."

"You think he'll go out this week?"

Charley tubed his lips thinking about it. "I'd say it's a long shot, I don't care how many kids he's got lined up. But hell, you never can tell, this may be the one." He grinned. "OK, now out with it. Ten bucks says he's told you he hasn't missed a year in four or five. Right?"

"Something like that."

Charley kept grinning. "Well that's Satch, he hasn't been anywhere, but that's how he thinks. It could have been, it should have been, it was. Like I said, how you going to argue with a guy like that. But back to your question. Nosir, Satchel Paige hasn't changed one damn iota."

After about an hour of practice and finishing up with two laps around the field Satch called them in around him.

"All right now, men, today's Wednesday; Friday we hit the road. Now if there's any problems, I want to hear them now, OK? And if you don't want to talk about them, phone me at home."

Charley was in my ear. "I still don't think he'll do it, but look at those kids and look at him. The son of a bitch might be pulling this thing off. Damn, I sure hope so."

CHAPTER  **8**

SATCH HAD BEEN on the stage in two or three medicine shows back in the forties to get publicity for his team and I wanted to know enough to be able to ask about them. At the public library the material wasn't hard to find and in a couple hours some of the pieces were beginning to fit together. The medicine shows and the circuits they rode turned out to be almost as big and as wild as the Negro Baseball League. And the names were as colorful; they were the ones Satch had rattled off at the Flamingo: Rabbit Foot, the Great Bartok Minstrels, Silas Green from New Orleans, and Snookum Nelson and His Creole Brothers.

I found out that the eastern troops started off from Florida heading north in the early spring following the strawberry, bean, tomato, and peanut crops north up through the Carolinas and Virginia until they hit Pennsylvania where they worked the coal miners. They stayed there until the weather began turning cool, then headed back south working the tobacco crop, and finally wrapped up the year in the Carolinas, Georgia, Alabama, and Mississippi with the cotton workers. With a fleet of trucks and sometimes a string of private rail cars, with special rooms for mixing the alcohol-laced tonics and cure-alls, they carried a cast as low as twenty and as high as a hundred. It was all hard to believe and too much to remember. I copied down the names, the dates, and the routes they'd taken, and the incredible casts: Red Skelton, Carmen Miranda, Bessie and her sister "Walking Mary" Smith, Mickey Rooney, Martha Raye, and Stepin Fetchit, and at least a dozen more. Each one had their own bright and brassy act, their own songs, their own jokes. And the three- to fifteen-piece bands backing them up, dressed in flashy satin tuxedos with candy-striped top hats and phosphorescent checkered vests, have left sounds out under the pecan and chinaberry trees that are still there.

Then I started reading the history. No one seemed to know exactly where the medicine show began in Europe back in the sixteenth and seventeenth centuries but all agreed it ended in this country around 1950 when the Food and Drug Administration ruled it illegal to sell medicine without a prescription. But the medicine show owners had not only seen the ban coming, they were ready for it. Quickly they traded their miracle tonics and their tambourines for lions and tigers and elephants, sno-cones, and high-wire acts; almost overnight they went into the circus business. And the more enterprising, charismatic pitchmen, who knew how to work a crowd, took it one or two or three steps further. Stripping down everything but their tents, trucks, and chairs, they struck out on the high-profit, low-overhead evangelical superhighway, where all they needed was a blue serge suit, a white shirt, and a Bible.

The ones that couldn't make the cut into evangelism wound up on the Interstate cutoffs running big-discount gas and souvenir stores. Still using the old five-inch-wide dynamite lettering—the width of a paint brush—and still looking like sideshows, there they are out on the fringe of show business selling pecan logs, fruitcakes, and memorabilia, but their big ticket item, the one in the center ring and the one you have to drag the kids past by the hair, is and always will be FIRE-WORKS! FIREWORKS! FIREWORKS!

◆

Later, back at the Twilight Zone Lounge, with the medicine show material fresh in my mind, I wanted to ask a hundred questions. But I didn't have to. All I had to do was listen to Satch and Charley talk about it.

Satch said they were paid five dollars a day for going on stage with Silas Green near Birmingham but Charley swore it was in Shreveport.

This irritated Satch; he didn't like being corrected. "Well it was down there someplace. What damn difference does it make?"

Charley backed down and Satch was off and running. "Yessir, Silas Green from New Orleans. Yowza! What a show. What a great goddamn show. Let me tell you who they had on the payroll. He had Bessie Smith. He had Mickey Rooney, Red Skelton. Hell old Ed McMahon was there at the end, he's what you call a peeler pitchman—you used to see them in Woolworth's selling potato peelers. And Lord, how that boy could sell."

Charley interrupted. "Tell him how he worked."

Satch shook him off; he had something else in mind. "Not now. Bo, you listen to this. Me and Charley here can fill you with more crap about the medicine shows than any one breathing. Hell, we might damn well be the last of the last. See, you live long enough you get to know stuff no one else knows. Ain't that right, Charley?"

Charley winced. "Ain't that the damn truth."

It was all working out. All I had to do was keep my mouth shut and let them ramble on down the roads. Earlier I'd tried taping Satch but he'd gone stiff when he saw the reel spinning. I'd even tried taking notes, but he kept watching to see what I was writing and it slowed him down and made him cautious. But now, knowing enough facts from the library, I knew all I had to do was ask the right questions and sit back and listen. I also knew there would be very little I'd be forgetting. The only thing I had to be careful of was not to try keeping up with them on the brew. "How about telling me what y'all did on these shows?"

It was the right question. Satch popped his hands and began rubbing them together and grinning like a miser. "You name it, we did it. Man we did everything. Hell, I'd sprinkle a handful of table salt out of an old Morton's box on the stage and I'd do one of those old vaudeville sand dances—you know slipping and sliding and spinning around. And that crazy crowd loved us. Then at the end Silas Green or Doc Bartok or whoever was playing Mister Interlocutor would tell them we were playing ball right down the road the next day and he wanted everyone in the audience to come out and see us."

Charley chimed in. "And they showed up too. Showed up in droves. People loved Silas Green and they'd do anything in the world for him. You should have seen the crowds at the games after we'd been on that show."

Satch took over. "Here's how it worked. We'd be sitting up there on the stage—I'd be Mister Bones and the MC would be Mister Interlocutor and he'd say, 'Mister Bones.' And I'd say 'Yes-sir Mis-ter In-ter-loc-u-tor.'

"And he'd say, 'Mister Bones, why don't you show the good folks your hesitation pitch.'

"And I'd say, 'Yes-sir Mis-ter In-ter-locutor.' And I'd get up and warm up with a ball and a catcher down on the other end of the stage. Then after I shook off a couple calls, I'd say, 'Here it comes.' I'd wind up and stop at the top and Mister Interlocutor would shout out, 'Hey Mis-ter Bones, what are you doing out there? Looks like you frozen and you hanging on a clothesline.'

"And I'd come back with, 'Mis-ter In-ter-loc-u-tor, I am hesitating right now so I can cog-i-tate on how I'm going to throw my Hes-i-ta-tion Pitch.' Then I'd cut it loose to the catcher and Mister Interlocutor and that crowd would go wild they'd be laughing so hard."

Charley was excited and broke in. "Satch! You're forgetting the Chicken pitch. Bo's got to hear that one."

Satch waved his hand. "No I ain't. I'm coming to it. Now here's how that one worked, and this was guaranteed to bring the house right down on its knees. Mister Interlocutor would shout out, 'That's wonderful, Mister Bones. You got anything else you want to show us?' See all this was free advertising for our ball game and I mean it paid off. Right, Charley?"

"Damn right, the next day it was standing room only."

Satch said, "OK, after I threw my Hesitation Pitch, Mister Interlocutor would say, 'That's wonderful, Mister Bones. That's wonderful. You got anything else like that for us?'

"I'd say, 'Yessir, Mister Interlocutor, I got my world-famous and internationally famous Chicken ball. This is the same, identical ball I threw for the king and queen of England and the king and queen of Spain. Them Spaniards ate it up.'

"He'd come back with, 'Chicken ball?'

"Then I'd roll my eyes and hambone and shuffle around a little. 'Yessir, those people over there in England and France and Spain and down there in old Italy lapped it up like red beans and rice.'

"And he'd say, 'Well, Mis-ter Bones. would you be so kind as to demonstrate this internationally famous Chicken ball?'

"And I'd say, 'Yessir, I'd be glad to.' OK, I'd look down the stage at my catcher and I'd shake off a few more signs until I got the right one. Then I'd nod my head up and down slow, you had to do it real slow, and I'd cross my eyes at the crowd and look crazy. Then I'd go into a long slow double windup. Then a triple windup. Then a quadruple windup. On the last loop of that quadruple I'd reach my left hand in my pocket and pull something out and slide it in my right. Then I'd fire it down the stage and out it would come, a rubber chicken as naked as a jaybird. And right on top of that the clarinet player would be making this chicken-squawking sound. Now you talk about something funny, those farmers fell right on out on that one. Bo, that crowd would be crying and down on their knees they'd be laughing so hard. I've never seen people laugh like that."

Charley raised his hand but Satch cut him off and continued, "And the minute they settled down Silas Green or the Great Bartok or whoever was up there would announce. 'All right I want every one of you to come out and see these fine boys play ball tomorrow right down the road from here. You'll see the signs on the barns and the fences and on the light poles. And if you ain't got a dime to get in, you hand them a label from a bottle of one of our fine products that we are just about ready to sell. And if you can't scratch that label off show them the whole bottle.'"

Satch continued, "See back then the medicine shows had all the stars. All of them. I mean ask yourself how's the blacks and some old redneck cracker going to get to see real show people unless they came to town and they were free. And Silas Green and Milton Bartok and Rabbit Foot had the stars, and that's what brought them in. Hell, what you talking about, you could look down the railroad tracks about first dark and here they'd be coming; kids on the rails, grown folks on the gravel, coming to see the show. And they'd have their shoes tied around their necks—see they were saving them for the show. And if the show was near say an overalls plant or a place where they made towels and sheets and pillowcases and things like that they'd bring it along as gifts. They'd bring cakes and pies and biscuits and sides of ham. And eggs too; fresh eggs. Because see, here's something you got to remember, this was in the forties and there wasn't much money around back then. Hell back on the farms and in them small towns they were still in the Depression. And I'll tell you the truth on that one, a lot of those folks were calling it the Compression."

Charley couldn't help himself, he cut in. "And they were good shows. Better than good, they were great."

Satch hated being interrupted. "I just said that. Hell yeah they were great. They may have been the greatest. You'd get to see stars. Real stars. Imagine looking up on stage and seeing someone like Carmen Miranda with those Brazil clothes and those banana hats. That gal caused a major sensation. See Bo, this was way back before television, back when radio was just getting on it's feet. Hell, most stations didn't have anything on but them hillbilly songs and fiddle scratchings coming out of

Nashville. Oh, and here's a few more stars they had back then, country stars: Roy Acuff was number one, then there was Ernest Tubbs and Little Jimmy Dickens, and old Minnie Pearl was out there too.

"Now here's a trick they'd all pull. When it came time for the sale—you know the medicine—Doc Milton Bartok or Silas Green would make each one of the chorus line run out in the crowd with two bottles. Two bottles, that's all. No more no less. Then the second we sold them we'd holler out, 'Sold out. Sold out' and go pounding back up the sawdust to get some more. Now right about here the crowd would start panicking. See, they're thinking we really had sold out and they'd buy that crap so fast it would make your head swim.

"Didn't I just mention Roy Acuff? Of course I did, Well let me tell you something about him that very few people know about. And you can write this down as a certified fact. Me and him were on the same show a couple times and became pretty good buddies there for a while. I bet you didn't know this, but Roy Acuff was one helluva ballplayer—I think he tried out—or hell, maybe he even played for the Yankees. But I let him work out with us a couple times and he had some nice moves and a smooth, sweet swing with that old timber. But what I'm getting to was the fact that he was one of the first singers to make a record. You check that one out for yourself. Anyhow, one night he said to me, 'Satch, I don't have any voice. I swear I don't. All I am is loud and all I am is clear. See, that's all it takes to get on the radio. I ain't got no voice and I ain't ever told anyone I had a voice.'"

Satch laughed. "I'll bet that skinny bastard sang 'Wabash Cannonball' a million times. That's all that crowd wanted to hear back then. That and anything old Jimmie Rodgers was singing. Now there was the boy that could write music and sing it. The TB got him in the end. Hell, I think he died right in the middle of a recording session. Next time you get a chance, you listen to 'Any Old Time.' There's not a country lick in it and it's beautiful. That's one of his all-time best."

Charley waited until Satch stopped to take a drink. "Tell him about Stepin Fetchit."

Satch snapped his fingers. "Right! Damn right. Thanks, Charley. I forgot all about him. Now here's something else most people don't even have a clue about. Be sure and write this down but if you get it wrong I'm going to skin your butt. Stepin Fetchit was two guys; one Stepin and one Fetchit. Hell, I knew both of them when they were out there. And funny! Man, what you talking about. They'd make you fall down they were so funny. But one of them died, I forget which one. I think it was Stepin. But maybe it was Fetchit and it was the other way around. Anyhow, one of them took both names and it set up like cement. So now he's out there running around someplace with both names. Hell, you can see him in the movies; he's a star. Got an old long funny face and he's always rolling his eyes and big footing it around acting like he don't have good sense. But he's still funny as hell, I declare he is. Yeah that boy could tell some stories too. He could tell some stories."

Charley nudged my arm. "Ain't you going to write some of this down?"

If there was one thing I was sure of it was there was no way I'd be forgetting any of this. "Nope, I think I can remember it."

We had another round and they rambled on about the days when the medicine shows and the mud circuses like Hagenback-Wallace and Clyde Beatty and the Cole Brothers and a dozen names I'd never heard were crossing the country. I sat back listening to the old stories and lies and feeling great about what I was going to write. I could always check out the baseball stats but the medicine show stuff was brand new and terrific. I wanted to get all I could while Satch and Charley were drinking together. And now that the American Legion kids and Charley were ready to travel, I had the perfect ending. I could see it now: Satch and Charley loading up the Ford wagon with the Coleman stove and the guitar and their equipment and checking to see that the kids had everything they needed. I could see the two cars pulling out with Satch's long hand in the air waving backward, and I could see them heading out Route 40 into the western sun. And if they didn't go? Well then, they just didn't go. It was still a good story, and maybe they'd go next year. But right now they had stopped talking about the medicine show and were talking about the old mud circuses. Satch looped his arm around Charley's shoulders. "You want to hear something sad? Sad. I mean sad. I saw an inside show in Cedar Rapids that would have dropped you to your knees. It was disgusting. The top rows were higher than the trapeze platforms. If I'm lying, I'm dying. Those goddamn people were looking *down* on the flyers. Now if that ain't pathetic, I'll eat it."

But then he cheered up. "Bo, there ain't nothing like a good old, outside in the dirt, old-fashioned mud circus. When that canvas gets wet it's the greatest soundboard for music in the world. See it smooths it out and holds it in tight. Then the crowd starts feeling it, and the acts feel the crowd, and then, whammo! Everything works and it starts building like a son of a bitch. You take an inside show in Madison Square Garden, and you can have a hundred elephants and four hundred performing tigers and John Phillip Sousa's whole damn brass band and it still feels like you're in a goddamn subway."

Satch rolled on about watching a mud circus setting up a big tent somewhere down in Arkansas. He was getting into close detail now and I was wishing I could write it down. "See, you use wooden stakes when you're out in the open, but if you're setting up on asphalt you've got to go with the steel. And you use half hitches and rolling hitches when you tie that thing down. And when you drop that canvas to move out you better damn well know what you're doing. It probably weighs four or five tons, and when it's wet you can double or hell even triple that. One guy working the king pole slot—that's the one right in the middle—got a rope around his neck and that fool got shot right up to the top. Fifty damn feet straight up. Fifty feet straight down. Killed him deader than a mullet."

I eased them away from the circus by asking about the stars

and the acts in the medicine shows. Charley started to say something but Satch raised one finger and was off again and running. "Remember that Sparky guy. Was that his last name?"

Charley said, "Damn right, Sparky. Lord, now that was one funny man."

Satch said, "Funny? What you talking about. That right there was the funniest man that ever drew breath. Bo, you listen to this. That man was so funny people would be falling out in the aisles. I mean it. Am I right or am I wrong, Charley?"

The beer was hitting Charley and his voice was slurring. "Right, Satch. That man was really funny. I can see him right now."

I'd thought the beer was hitting Satch but I was wrong. It was hyping him up and his eyes were glistening. "I'll tell you exactly how funny that man was. Now first of all Bo you got to keep this straight, the crowd back then was still segregated. But a lot of the medicine shows segregated them down the middle. You know, whites on one side and blacks on the other. None of that blacks in the back and up in the crow's nest bullshit. The medicine men, they knew how to work things so everybody got a chance to see everything. But the high point every night was old Sparky. Damn I can't come up with his last name. But it was one of those straight names like Smith or Brown. Something straight like that.

"Anyhow, now this is something you got to know and it's something they don't teach you in school. A black man or a black woman laughs different than a white one. I swear it. They get looser and jump around and hug one another. Then lot of times they'll flop right down on the ground and roll around like they do in church. I swear to God if that ain't gospel. Right, Charley?"

Charley nodded, all he could get in was, "You right, Satch."

Satch went on. "So what old Silas Green and Bartok and the others would do was they'd put these heavy-duty reinforced seats on the black side and the regular seats on the white. If I'm lying, I'm dying. See, because a black man or woman will tear up a regular seat. And if you get some old fat black mama going she'll ruin two or three of them regulars. So you got to go with the heavy duties.

"Anyhow this Sparky was the number one funniest man I've ever seen and I have seen some funny people running around. See, everything he did was funny. He'd walk funny. Sit funny. Eat funny. Every move he made was funny. So by the time he was into his act you were already cracking up before he even got started. Lord, I can see that rascal now. God, he was good. None of his jokes were what you'd call showstoppers. Hell, right now if you put a pistol to my head I wouldn't be able to come up with a single one. And if you printed them up on a piece of paper and read them out loud they still wouldn't be nothing. I mean nothing. But it was the way he told them that was so damn funny. Man, he would tear you up.

"Bo, a lot of comedians need a crowd to be in front of to be funny. But not Sparky. He liked the crowd all right and the crowd loved him. But see he didn't really need that crowd the way these birds on TV need them. Hell, you watch Johnny Carson. If he tells a joke and not enough people laugh he'll goose his lips out and go into a pout. I mean it. And that buddy of his, that Rickles guy, hell, he'll start crying right there on the camera." He laughed. "And you know yourself, that man is just too ugly to cry in public like that. But Sparky was different. I've seen him walk out in a cornfield or a cotton field or down the side of a damn drain ditch all by himself and just be cutting the fool for nobody but himself."

Satch lit a cigarette from the butt of the one he was finishing. "You know something, I guess I'm a little like old Sparky. I mean I like the crowd and I want them to have a good time out there. But most of the time when I'm doing things, you know like shuffling along or doing stuff in slow motion or little funny peppers with the ball, I'm doing that for myself. Yeah, I guess I am a little like old Sparky, because I don't like people crowding in on me too close. I like to get off by myself like that."

The beers were hitting all of us pretty good when I asked them to tell me some more about what they did up on stage. Satch nonchalantly made a long reach over to the next table and picked up a saltcellar. He unscrewed the top and stepping out on the floor began pouring it in a little circle around him. Shooting his cuffs to free his wrists he flourished his lighted cigarette and slid it behind his ear, then he went into a soft shuffling sand dance.

Rudolph hollered over. "Dammit, Satch, you ain't ruining my floors now are you?"

Satch tipped his hat on a hard medicine show angle and easing his hands into his pockets kept on dancing. "Rudolph, all I'm doing is putting a high polish on them."

He swooped and slipped and minced back and forth in front of us. Then sliding his right foot in behind his left and popping his hands together he did a double spin. "I used to do three of these. Now I'm down to two. But Bo, I don't want you writing about that."

I wanted him to keep going. "Let me see that cakewalk again. I still can't get over that one."

Satch pulled Charley on to his feet. "Come here, boy. Let's show this cracker something."

They pushed their hats down on their noses until they were covering their eyes and Satch began snapping his fingers like castanets. "Now watch our legs. It's all in the legs. And you got to keep your body back like this. Way back."

He began singing and Charley, falling in behind as his shadow, joined in

Who's as sweet as a Georgia Peach?
That's Sweet Georgia Brown.

They rared back and with their elbows up and straight out they moved across the floor high stepping as high as they could reach. Then flailing their hands like fan blades and pumping their arms for balance they kept on singing.

She can dance and she can sing.
She can do most anything,
Georgia claimed her, Georgia
named her, Sweet Georgia Brown.

The crowd at the bar whistled and applauded and someone sent over a round.

After the room calmed down and Satch and Charley had caught their breath I asked them if they ever got to know any of the medicine show owners. Charley started to speak but Satch played on through. "Well I only knew a couple of them. And I really didn't get to know them too well. See, it's hard getting to know people like that. It's like they say, they can know you but you'll never really know them."

He talked about the Great Bartok, who left the medicine business and bought out the Hunt Brothers Circus. "For my money, Milton Bartok was the best man out there. Next to him everyone else was back in the shade. But even the ones back in the shade were terrific. Because you are talking about some stiff competition. I mean those boys and gals went at it.

"Bartok only worked about an hour a night but that was all he needed. That boy could read a crowd like they were written in neon because he knew how to pitch and when to pitch. And he knew how to get them up on their feet so they could get at their wallets and pocketbooks, because you can't sell them nothing while they're sitting down. He told me once he had them on their feet they'd start sounding like a beehive. Then they'd change keys and he'd feel like he'd hooked onto a big fish and he had to play it until it was tired and then reel them in. See, that's what you've got to know. When to wait and when to sell. That might sound simple but that is one complicated move. Man, you got to know something to pull that one off. But the smart ones like Bartok knew exactly when they were ready. Not too early. Not too late.

"Now a lot of them had that old tried-and-true Billy Graham back and forth and side to side pendulum move. Graham wears those dark long lapel jobs, and he's skinny enough, I guess he does look a little like a pendulum. They claim if you did it right it would hypnotize a crowd. I never swallowed that one but I guess I believed some of it. But I sure as hell believed everything else. But anyhow, Bartok would wait until Sparky had them all loosened up and ready, then he'd go into his spiel and start making his signs.

"Hold it, let me back up here. I've skipped something that's pretty important and pretty damn complicated. When this crowd came into town they'd send in a couple front-runners who'd read it. That's right, read it, read that town the way you'd read a road map or a damn newspaper. See, they'd check the signs at the city limits, you know you've seen them: Rotarians, Kiwanis, Lions, Elks, clubs like that. Then the churches; how many Catholics, how many Baptists, how many Pentecostals were out there. That sort of stuff. Then they'd hit the department stores and check the prices and talk to a few people on the street and get a good grip on the accents. Hell, you give those boys and girls a couple hours and they'd know that town inside and out. And the girls would hit the ladies' rooms. God knows what they found out in there but that's where they'd go. There and the beauty shops."

Charley interrupted. "Lot of the crowd went into politics. They're out there right now reading towns and telling the politicians what to say and who to say it to. Ain't that right, Satch?"

"Damn right that's right." Satch bobbed his head up and down. "And it makes sense because those boys and gals were smart. Smart as whips and razor sharp. When Bartok took that stage he knew exactly who he was talking to. I mean ex-act-ly. First he'd throw out a few lines to let the Rotarians know he was one of them. I forget the lines now but then he'd do the Lions, then the Optimists. Yeah, now I remember one. 'Deep down dead level,' that was the secret code for the Masons. Then he'd let them know he was a member of the Elks and the Kiwanis and the Knights of Columbus until he had them all.

Then he'd raise three or four fingers behind his head for the sign of the Moose and the sign of the Elks and touch them together in a little steeple, about like this, for the Ku Klux Klan.

"And, get this, he didn't wastes five seconds on this because he was doing it while he was introducing the show. That rascal was slick. He had them believing he was in every club and church in town and that he was Irish, German, Spanish, and Italian. Anything you could name, that's what he was. Hell, that fool would dust his face with a little bit of brown powder and you couldn't even tell if he was black or white or if he was running around with red Indian in his blood. If I'm lying, I'm dying.

"And there was an old gal, Madame Rosemary, who could read heads and work roots, and she had her a little room in the back where she handled the women. She couldn't say she belonged to the clubs because they were all male but she could solid tell them what was going on in the kitchens and what was going on in the bedrooms. Hell, she'd get them back in that little canvas room and sell them nine and ten kinds of love potions and romance powders. And something else, she kept four or five jars of human parts in alcohol or formaldehyde or something and she'd show them those things and give them little lectures. I mean that old gal would get down in the dirt and get raw."

Satch stood up, excusing himself, and headed for the men's room. The minute Charley and I were alone he grabbed my arm. "Bo, I'd be the last person in the world to be telling you how to write this piece but I sure wish you'd try and get in that if it wasn't for Satchel Paige there wouldn't have been any Jackie Robinson. Maybe you'll have to tone it down and say it would have been a helluva lot harder for Jackie if Satch hadn't gone on ahead of him. But you be sure and get something like that in there. Because Satch is exactly like old Sparky up on that stage—he plowed that field first and he got the public ready for anything and that's when they brought in Jackie. Now you got to agree with that."

I said I did, and I meant it.

Satch came back snapping his fingers and pointing his pistol finger at me. "Bo, I got a good one for you. You ever heard of dinging?"

"Nope, afraid not."

He tapped Charley's shoulder. "How about you stud?"

"Not me either."

Satch was off and running as he sat back down. "That's when a circus balloon salesman wraps the string around a baby's finger. Now you talk about some fast hands and nimble fingers—those boys and girls are magicians. And if you didn't buy that balloon you had one helluva time prying it loose from that kid. Because that little son of a bitch is going to be screaming until the cows come home." He laughed. "That's one of the slickest moves out there."

For the rest of the afternoon all Charley would say was "damn right, Satch," and "you right about that, Satch," and "you tell him, Satch." There was no doubt about it, Satch had found a sideman who wasn't going to give him any trouble, and they were going to get along fine.

It was five when the happy hour crowd started packing in around the bar for the half-price drinks. Satch said he had to pick Lahoma up from her job at the bakery and he wanted to beat the heavy traffic. He stood up and finishing his beer pointed the bottle at Charley. "Listen here, I don't want you throwing to second from your knees anymore. Puts too big a strain on your back and you're too heavy in the rear for that. Just raise up until you're comfortable and let her fly."

"OK, Satch, all you have to do is tell me what you want. I'm not going to give you a lick of trouble. Just tell me what you want."

SATCH DROPPED ME off at the library and I went straight to the nonfiction section and sitting on the floor in the stacks began pulling out some of the old books on the medicine shows. I also pulled out a kid's book, *America's Most Famous Heroes.* I knew I'd never find Satch in it but I wanted to see who had made the cut.

It was a big, beautiful, predictable book published in 1950 and began right where it was supposed to begin with George Washington crossing the Delaware. He was followed by Ben Franklin and his electric kite and the signers of the Declaration of Independence standing around the table at Philadelphia. Still sitting there in the aisle, I flipped through the Revolutionary War and Civil War generals, picked up Thomas Alva Edison and Henry Ford, and ended with MacArthur returning to the Philippines and Eisenhower landing on the beach at Normandy. The athletes sandwiched in between the generals, politicians, and inventors were Christy Mathewson, Ty Cobb, Babe Ruth, Lou Gehrig, Jim Thorpe, and Jesse Owens; there was no mention of Satch or Josh Gibson or Cool Papa Bell or anyone from the Negro League. There was no mention of the Negro League.

But then, when I was pushing the book back on the shelf

something happened. It slipped and fell to the floor, wide open at the middle pages. There was Buffalo Bill Cody in brilliant color on one page and Buffalo Bill Cody in brilliant color on the facing page.

The printer's date was 1899, and Cody in his tasseled leather and flowing beard was up on his rearing white horse waving his white hat with one hand and a smoking forty-four in the other. Indians, cowboys, Conestoga wagons, and riders, and flags of all nations were whirling around him in an Apache circle while the announcement across the top in oversize dynamite lettering read:

My Last and Final Appearance
in the Saddle.

No one had stopped the artist from stacking a hundred thousand people in the bleachers.

The poster on the opposite page, stretching into the same clouds and the mountains in the distance, was posthumous. In the middle of the circle and the waving crowd, the ghost of Cody sat tall in his silver saddle with his white hat raised to the sky.

Let My Show Go On.

Buffalo Bill Cody was a showman and ringmaster but with his heavy endorsement of Kickapoo Indian Medicine, and the steep percentage he was taking off the top, he was probably a bonafide class-A fraud. But in some odd way that I couldn't put my finger on he reminded me of Satch. But Satch could play ball like no one else; I didn't know what Buffalo Bill had actually done except shoot a few tired old buffaloes and make a lot of money.

Babe Ruth might be closer. He'd been raised in an orphanage and there was no doubt about it, he was a great pitcher and great hitter. But there was always something of the barroom yokel in him that he was never able to shake. Jim Thorpe and Jesse Owens and the others had the ability but none had the range, the humor, and not one of them came even close to Satch's flamboyant character or his incredible charisma.

But it seemed as if there had to be someone out there that was a little like him. I went back through the book looking over Lindbergh, Franklin Roosevelt, Will Rogers, and Mark Twain, and every one of them, on my lunatic rating sheet, was missing the cut by a mile.

Will Rogers and Mark Twain seemed the closest but only for a moment. For while Rogers and Twain had had interesting lives and went on to talk and act and write about it, Satch had never stopped living it. What I was arriving at was something I was in the process of discovering: there was no one you could compare him to because there simply had never been anyone out there like him.

The idea of comparing him to Cody or Twain or Will Rogers didn't make sense and I knew I had to forget it and make some notes on the medicine shows. I also knew I couldn't spend much time with him on that either, because at any moment he might just get fed up, ask for the rest of his money, and like one of his famous fastballs simply disappear. I had to get him back talking about baseball and the old Negro Leagues and I had to do it fast.

"OK, MY BIRTH certificate says Mobile, Alabama, 1908, and I ain't going to argue with that one." We were back at the Twilight Zone Lounge and he was talking about his early years. "My dad was a gardener but he liked to call himself a landscaper, he even had calling cards printed up saying that, Landscaper. But no matter what he called it he still couldn't rub two dimes together. I mean we never had enough money and I'm talking about a family of eleven. Anyhow, I was number seven and we were all jammed together in an old four-room shotgun house. Y'all have shotguns back in Columbia?"

"Oh yeah, they're still with us."

"Then you know what I'm talking about. One room right behind the other. You could stand on the front porch and bounce a basketball right on through and out to the backyard. Oh yeah. And you take a dog scratching fleas on the front porch, hell, he'd be vibrating those boards right through every damn one of them rooms. Anyhow, we didn't have much money, because there wasn't much money around in them days. So we all worked. The first thing I did to raise money was sell bottles to the bootleggers."

I interrupted. "Me too. That's what I did."

"Is that right? Well hell, let's hold it right here. Let's talk about bottles then. How much you get for them?"

"A penny for half pints, two for pints, four for quarts."

"Right, there wasn't no fifths back then. Now tell me where'd you go to get them?"

"Trash piles, men's rooms, ladies' rooms, in the backs of alleys."

"Shee-it, that was my territory. That's where I was hanging out. I was an authority on them damn Mobile alleys and men's rooms. Hold it, Bo, I don't like to rush you like this but this is something I've got to do. I need me a favor right now. I need a little money for tonight."

My heart sank as I opened my wallet and slid out his ten hundred dollar bills. Now there would be no way of holding onto him. But he raised his hand. "No, don't give me all that now. Just two hundred. If I've got a thousand I'll spend a thousand."

He smiled but it wasn't funny. "I know my pattern. I know exactly what I'll do. You just hang on to the rest of that for now. I'll let you know when I need it."

I creased the two bills together and pushed them over. He slid them in his shirt pocket. "Thanks, Bo. Tell you what, if I start yakking about something you already know about, you cut me off and I'll push on through. OK with you?"

"Fine with me."

"Now back to the bottles. You remember the old spider-web?"

"No, I missed that one."

He whistled, "A real beauty. It looked like it was cracked because it had this web built into the glass. How about the waffle ridge? You got to remember that one?"

"Yeah, that one I remember."

"That was the one you could get a grip on." He lit a cigarette and shook the match out. "OK, that's enough about bottles for now, let's get back to Mobile. Well we were poor, no doubt about that. Hell, I don't remember us having electricity until I came back from the Industrial School. Had those old kerosene lamps that you couldn't see doodley-squat by. You make a mistake and turn one of those things over and your house was gone. But we always had plenty of food and plenty of fish and Momma kept a big garden up. Ever heard of the Mobile Bay Jubilee?"

"This is the first time."

"Happens two or three times a year when something happens to the water. It gets too much salt or too much something or maybe it's not enough and the fish go crazy and start jumping up on the banks. Whenever it happened the police and the fire department would run around town with their sirens screaming so everybody would know they were jumping. Anyhow, we'd go down there with washtubs and croaker sacks and every pot in the house to pick them up. Some would be as big as your hand and some would be as big as your arm. Hell, I saw one big one jump up in a damn tree, up in the branches. Now that's something I'll never forget—a fish in a tree. Wish I had a picture of that one.

"I guess we didn't have anything to play with back then, no balls or bats or gloves or anything like that. As a matter of fact we used to rub dirt in our faces to keep the gnats off, that's how bad off we were. Anyhow, I got to throwing rocks and I got good pretty good. I could hit birds on the wire, big ones and little ones. I could hit anything because I had that natural arm action where I didn't have to aim. I just let it flow. I'll bet I threw them rocks the same way I pitched ball from then on. See, once you have the action and it's working for you there's no reason why you're going to be changing.

"Anyhow, we had to go to school through the white section every day, and every day we'd have the same damn fistfight. But I got smart fast. Real fast. What I'd do was just step back, way back, and I'd let them rocks do the talking for me. I hit so many crackers they had to call the law."

He laughed, "I guess right in there was when I really started pitching because those boys backed off and from then on they left us alone. I'll tell you something else, those fights made me a big man with my buddies and a big man in the neighborhood instead of some little old nigger black trash. Yeah, that all came out of chunking rocks."

He asked if I knew where he got the nickname Satch. I said I thought I did but I wanted to hear his version.

"Well, when I was about seven or eight I decided there wasn't a helluva lot of money or any future in selling bottles to the bootleggers. So I got out of that and went down to the train station and started hustling bags but that wasn't much better. Hell, it was worse. All I could make was a dime at a time and sometimes you had to carry that thing four or five blocks. So I rigged up a pole and some ropes and made a kind of sling so I could carry three or four at one time. Now see I was only seven or eight but I was already tall. Some of the guys claimed I looked like a telephone pole or a stork or an ostrich. So when they saw me carrying that pole and that rope mess they began hollering out that I looked like a satchel tree. And right in there was where it started, and from then on, that was me 'Satchel.'

"I guess I was closer to my momma than my dad; she was the one that kept that big old family together. It seemed like Dad was gone a lot. I didn't see him much and we never seemed to talk too much either. But a couple times I remember him saying 'Leroy, it looks to me like you got your mind set on being a baseball player instead of a landscaper.'

"And I'd say 'Yessir, I wouldn't mind that at all.' I guess he was a lot smarter than I thought he was.

"OK now I'll tell you about the first real pitching I did. It was for Wilbur Hines, who was the coach over at the W. H. Council School in Mobile; they were in one of those little old raggedy-ass local leagues no one had every heard of. I guess I was just over ten about then but I was tall and I could throw, and hell, I could hit. One thing about me, and you can count on this, I could always play ball. Anyhow Wilbur Hines started me out in the outfield and I played out there for about half the season. But one day the team we were playing knocked out all our pitchers in the first inning, so Hines waved me in and asked me if I could shut them down.

"And that's what I did, I shut their butts down. Here I am only a little over ten but I could really throw that fastball. And listen to this, you'd think a kid that young would be scared to death out there on that mound but, Bo, I was as cool as cucumber.

"See, I knew I was good and I knew I could get that ball by anyone. I swear to God, that's exactly how I felt. The first three batters I faced I sat down one, two, three—three strikeouts. The next three the exact same thing; strikeout, strikeout, strikeout. And I kept that up for eight more innings. I didn't give up a single hit. How about that, my first time out and I get me a shutout. Shutout hell; if you take those pitchers out of the first inning I had me a Don Larsen perfect no-hitter. Man, I was on top of the world on that mound. I'd found me a home out there and I wasn't ever going to climb down. Now that's exactly how my first game went. Old Hines slapped me on the back and said, 'Son from now on you're our number one pitcher.' And that's where it all began.

"So you see, I started off like a house afire and I was doing everything I could to keep pouring on the gasoline. There was no one on the southside who could throw as fast and had my control, and when those kids who were about my age stepped in the box and I wound up with my Trouble ball they'd wet their pants and cry. Hell, what you talking about, a lot of them wouldn't even get in the box, that's how scared they were."

Satch talked on about how he got caught stealing from a five-and-dime store and the store called in the truant officer. "I'll tell you the exact day of that little episode, it was the twenty-fourth of July, 1918, and you can check it out. That's the day they committed me to the Industrial School for Negro Children at Mount Meigs, Alabama.

"But I'll tell you the gospel truth on that one, the Mount wasn't bad, it wasn't bad at all. What they did there was try and find out what you liked to do and then they let you do it.

Things like singing and playing in the drum and bugle corps and baseball. I told them I wanted to go out for baseball and I wanted to pitch. And I told them I wanted to do some singing. And they let me do everything.

"Hell, I even did pretty well in school. So I'd say that as far as the Mount was concerned it was pretty good for me. Strike that, make that very good for me, because they let me pitch and do everything I wanted.

"Well I stuck around there until I was fifteen or sixteen, and all this time I'm growing like a weed. I was up to six feet, three and a quarter inches. But the catch to that was I only weighed 140. The boys on the team began calling me Crane; they said I looked like a crane. Funny, I'd been a stork down at the railroad and an ostrich, now I was a crane. Did I tell you about wearing all those stockings to make my legs look bigger?"

I told him he had and he went on.

"Well being that tall and skinny wasn't all bad, as a matter of fact it was perfect for pitching. The coach showed me how to kick up my foot so it looked like it was blacking out the sky. Later on I wrote FASTBALL in big letters on the sole so every batter I faced got to take a good look at it. And Coach taught me to swoop my arm around so it looked like I was letting the ball go when my hand was right in the batter's face. And he taught me something else, something I used from then on, and it's something I don't think I ever told anyone. Well maybe I did.

"Anyhow it's this, you don't watch a batter's shoulders or his eyes or where his hips are pointing. You watch his knees. Coach said it was just like a bullfighter watching a bull. When he sees that movement with the knees he knows exactly what the next move's going to be. That's a fact, and that's what I've been using and I'm still using.

"I guess I was about seventeen when they finally let me out of the Mount and I headed back to Mobile. When I got there all my brothers and sisters had grown up. But see, by now. even though I was one of the youngest, I was bigger and taller than every one of them.

"Now let me try and get these years straight in here. This has got to be in 1923 or '24, right in there, because that was when my brother Wilson was pitching for the Mobile Tigers. Well one day he took me to the field to watch them work out, and I stretched out on the top row in the stands and started looking everything over.

"Anyhow, this turned out to be my lucky day because that was the day the manager—I forget his name now—was out there hitting balls off kids who were trying out as pitchers. I watched a couple or three and everything these kids were throwing, that guy would slap right up against the wall. OK, so when the last kid walked off I dropped down out of the stands and told him I wanted him to try me out. OK, so he asked me where I'd been pitching but I didn't want to say 'the Mount,' so I said, 'Oh around. All around. All over the state.' I know he didn't believe me. Then I told him I was Wilson's brother and he said, 'OK warm up a little and I'll take a look and see what you got.'

"So I went out to the mound, shook my arm loose and whistled in a few fast ones. Then I called out. 'OK, mister, I'm ready when you are.' So he got in the box and I whipped that ball by him so fast he didn't even see it. I remember he was grinning when he stepped back in and said, 'Now that ain't too bad. Let me see some more.'

"And brother, that fellow saw some more. He saw some of my very best fastballs. I whistled ten or eleven of them in there and every one was the same ball. A fastball. But I kept moving it around a little to keep him from getting set and I had him swinging late on every one of them. So here I am right out of reform school and out on this mound in Mobile and I'm saying to myself, Satch, if you have to face three guys like this in an inning all I'm going to be needing is nine pitches."

"See Bo, I'm green as grass and I wasn't even studying shaving but I was pumped up and my juices were flowing and I'll tell you exactly what I said to myself. I said, nine pitches a side times nine innings. And I said, Satch, all you need is eighty-one pitches for a whole damn game.

"Let's hold the phone right here. I don't want you getting the idea I was bragging or anything like that. See, I was saying exactly what I knew I could do. And you know something, Bo, that's the way it's been with me all the doggone life. I always knew I could get that ball by any batter you put out there in front of me."

He laughed. "Later on I told some reporter that if Babe Ruth and Lou Gehrig had to face me back when they were breaking all those records I could have knocked a few points off of those big fat lifetime averages. And hell, I meant it. I was laughing when I said it, but I was not joking, I meant every word I said. See, hitting the ball is one thing, but hitting against a fastball pitcher who can put it where he wants it every time is a whole 'nother story.

"Anyhow, back at Eureka Gardens, the manager gave me a dollar and told me to come back with Wilson the next day. That was the first dollar I'd made playing ball. I wish I'd framed that thing because I don't know when I'd been so happy.

"Wilson and I played for the Tigers for a couple months and we were real good together. See, he could throw it harder than me but he didn't stick with the game the way I did. And besides he didn't want to leave Mobile. Hell, I didn't care where I went as long as I could play ball. And I was willing to work at it, and practice hard and study like a damn madman. Everything I needed to get better I did. But right there, that day with the Tigers and that first paper dollar bill, was where my career began."

He took a long pull on his beer. "And it's been going like that for me ever since."

I asked if he remembered what kind of year he had that first year, and he said, "Yeah, I remember almost everything about it. That's something else I got, I got me a first-class memory that won't quit. I won at least thirty and I only lost one. But see, here's the catch to that one. Even though I was winning every game I pitched, this was semipro ball and there never has been any money in that, especially for the blacks. Hell, you break it all down and it was only a couple steps up from sandlot. I tell you what I was getting, I was getting a dollar a game. So you figure that one out, you win twenty games and you get twenty dollars. And if they didn't have that dollar, they'd give you a keg of lemonade or something like that. Hell, if you didn't have a steady job or some money in your pocket from someplace you were going to starve playing semipro.

"So if I was going to make any money I knew I had to keep my options open and I had to keep looking around. OK, by this time the rest of the town knew about me and every team breathing wanted to sign me up. But see, they didn't have any money either. I guess I could have gone back down to the train station and made another dollar a day but I knew I was never going to do that crap again.

"But the next year I got my big break and signed up with the Chattanooga Black Lookouts, one of the big teams in the old Negro Southern League. They were going to pay me fifty dollars a month. Nowadays you can't get a decent meal for that kind of money but back in 1926 that was big-time money. Big-time. They wanted to sign up Wilson too but he said no. He wasn't going to leave home. Too bad too, because he was one of the very best. That was a shame he didn't come along. We could have had some great times together.

"Well I got to Chattanooga and I didn't even have a suitcase. Everything I had was in an old brown paper sack from the grocery store, you know the kind. All I had was an extra pair of pants and a few pieces of underwear and socks and two measly shirts. I wrapped everything in one of the shirts, tied it up by the sleeves, and shoved it in and that was it. That was my traveling gear, and that's how I hit Chattanooga, Tennessee.

"Right away, Alex, that's the guy who signed me up, let me start against Birmingham and I didn't let him down. We won one to nothing, a shutout. How about that, a shutout in my first game. I only gave up two hits. Then I faced them again a couple days later and did the same thing, only this time three hits. Nothing big, just little bingles that dropped in over the infielders. Alex got me off to one side and gave me a five dollar bill and told me to go have some fun. If I'm not mistaking that was the first five dollar bill I'd ever seen. Maybe I'd seen one but that was the first one I'd earned.

"Guess where I headed? Right for the damn poolroom. And guess what happened? They cleaned old Satch's clock. They set me up until we got the money up, then they shut me down. I always figured I was pretty good at nine-ball and eight-ball but those sleepy-eyed Chattanooga sharpies played me like the biggest fish in the Tennessee River.

"Now I'm going to give you a quick tip about pool sharks. Here's how you can spot them. They don't carry two-piece sticks the way they do in the movies. And they don't miscue every four or five shots the way they do in the movies. They do a little something that you do not see in the movies. Here's what they do and here's how you can spot them. You watch where they put that chalk in between shots. Every doggone one of them slides it in their pocket. Now the reason for that is a shark, I'm talking about a real shark, who's going to be play-ing four and five hours a day, is going to be looking after his feet and he's going to be looking after his legs. See, when you play that many hours that's what gives out first. So that scutter is doing everything he can to save himself some steps. So next time you play, you watch where that guy is putting his chalk. Makes sense doesn't it?"

"Yeah, it sure does. I'm going to remember that one." I didn't want him going off on another tangent. "Satch, let me hear some more about the Negro League."

"OK, Bo. Sorry I got off the track like that. Now first off, the Negro League was about ten times better than playing semipro in Mobile, maybe twenty or thirty times. And it was much better ball. If I had to make a prediction for back in then, I'd say that in the thirties and the forties, any team in the Negro League could beat any white major league team any day of the week and twice on Sunday. Now that's going to sound to you like a strong statement. But that's exactly how good we were. I mean now, why in the hell, would I lie about it. It was true. Dead true. Now let me explain this and clear it up.

"Bo, as a white man, you got to face some pretty hard facts of life. A black man is always going to be faster than a white man. Not just some of the time, I'm talking all the time. I'm talking always. A white man running against a black man just ain't going to cut it. You might as well ask a bulldog to try and keep up with a greyhound. Let's put it this way, how many whites do you see out there running the one-hundred and the two-hundred yard dashes these days? Very few and getting fewer every day. You check out the Olympics and you'll see very few whites out there from this country in the dashes. OK, you'll still see a couple from England and Scandinavia but that crowd don't count, they never win anything anyway. But see, we were built for speed and we were built for endurance. Now I'll give you another prediction—twenty or thirty years from now there won't be a single white running back in professional football. I'm probably sticking my neck out too far on that one, but I'd lay even money on it. I swear I would."

He waggled his hands and made himself change directions. "Hell, you don't want to be hearing all this bullshit. Let me get back to Chattanooga. Now where was I? Oh yeah, I was fixing to tell you about those first days up there. Listen to this. On our first trip out of town we went to Memphis in an old bus with worn-out springs and the damn bushings about to fall out. That thing bounced and shimmied like it had the tremens. I mean everything was falling out of the racks. One old boy brought his guitar along and all that shaking and vibration had that thing humming all the way across Tennessee. And that kind of crap will give you a four-day migraine. Now this bus was built for kids and it had those short seats so, hell, you couldn't even lean back. All you could do was sit up straight. So there was no way you were going to sleep unless you were one of those yoga guys who do it on nails. I mean this was rough on everyone, but how about me with my six feet three and a quarter. Like where am I going to put my legs? Where am I going to put my arms? I wound up sitting with my hands in my damn pockets, that's the only place I could find where I could put them.

"But we were young and green and I guess a lot of it didn't matter that much. Anyway, as we're pulling into Memphis I'm sitting there like a fool smiling away thinking about the nice hot shower and clean sheets coming up and a real bed I can stretch out on. Anyhow, we grind and rattle right on by the hotels and right on by the motels and we keep on going until we're out in the dark all the way out to the ballpark. We finally stop and Alex hollers for us to get out because the bus has to go back. And I holler out, 'Hey, where we supposed to be sleeping? We can't sleep out there.' And he hollers back, 'Come on, Satch, you'll get used to it.' So I say, 'I'm going to get used to sleeping on the ground?' Now Bo, I was saying this part to myself. Because I'm so glad to be here I can hardly stand it and I'm not going to be giving anybody any trouble.

"Well that first night we had to sleep right down on the dirt with our suitcases for pillows. And you talk about a hard night, that was it. Hard. I thought I'd never get to sleep. Lucky it was warm and didn't rain because right in there at this time, that was all old Alex could afford. Anyhow in the morning I was one sore son of a bitch but so was everyone else. But we shook it off and got us something hot to eat and we were off and running.

"But old Alex was right, we got used to it. After a few days of this we had a little money and he started getting us in the Negro hotels and then once in a while we'd be staying with his friends. See, when you go south and there ain't no hotels or motels for blacks, it gets pretty rough. I mean Alex had to really plan everything close. Where we going to stay? Where we going to eat? Where we going to make a phone call? Hell, you had to plan where you could go to the goddamn bathroom. Most of us took a leak out the back door of the bus but there's other things you have to do beside taking a piss and you know that was always going to be a problem.

"Later on I took the plunge and got me a big old Cadillac

with yellow wooden spokes and brass hubcaps and a silver naked gal leaning into the breeze for a radiator cap. One of those big old Al Capone twelve-cylinder jobs that looked like a locomotive and drank gas like a tractor. Man that boat had everything: a roller shade on the back window, velvet curtains on the sides, and a little speaker phone in case you had a chauffeur. And that old deep breather had a running board wide enough for me to sleep on. If I'm lying, I'm dying. What I'd do was park on an angle so I'd be tipped in at the car. That way I wouldn't fall off in case I moved. Anyhow, one night I'm lying out there with a cold beer chording my guitar with my little feather pillow up on the fender. Hell, I don't have any idea where I was, but I was looking up at the Milky Way and remembering how far I'd come and how fast I'd got there. All the way from throwing rocks in Mobile and the reform school to playing professional baseball and sending money home to Momma and owning the longest Cadillac on the road and I was thinking, now man this is the exact kind of life I was cut out for. This has got to be the top of the line and I was loving every minute of it. All of a sudden I just rared back, took a deep breath and I shouted, 'HOO-RAY!'

"I guess that right there says it all. I was happy out there. Man, I was so happy. I mean really happy. You got to remember when I was back in Mobile I was just another little old raggedy-ass trash nigger putting that nasty dirt on my face to keep the gnats off, and I was heading nowhere but downhill in a hurry. I mean if I hadn't been able to throw that ball the way I did I guarantee I'd have wound up in jail or in some kind of big-time trouble that I'd never have gotten out of. Later on when things got too rough to handle I could always look back at that night out there sleeping on the running board and hollering out HOO-RAY! Yeah, that was sure nice."

He was quiet for awhile, then he said, "Let me tell you the kind of food we'd eat out on the road. It'll give you something to write about. Hell, I'll even give you the recipe. It ain't no secret. First of all it was pretty simple but when you're out there working as hard as we were everything tastes good. What I'd do was get my Coleman going and heat up the frying pan and toss in a little grease. Then I'd cut up some onions real fine and toss them in and stir them around till they were brown. OK, then I'd put in my hamburger, maybe two pounds. And you want that ground chuck, that's got a little fat in it. Lean meat won't do it. Then when that gets brown and looks like its getting done I'd add in a big can of Campbell's Pork & Beans and a number two can of Del Monte tomatoes. Hamburger and beans, hell, that's all it was and that's what we called it. Lord, I can close my eyes right now and I can taste it.

"Of course when you're young and limber like that and out on the road and working as hard as we were anything tasted good. And every now and then I'd cook up some rice. If you can cook rice right you can cook anything. Because you can add all kinds of things to it; black beans, red beans, salmon, eggs, chopped-up Vienna Sausage or bologna, or anything. You name it and you can mix it with rice. Same with grits. But with grits you've got to go with the yellow kind, white grits ain't nothing. You know what they say about white grits? They say a dog will eat exactly a pound of white grits and then he'll shit exactly a pound of white grits. There's not one ounce of anything in them that'll stick to your ribs. That's why you got to go with yellow.

"Then lot of times for dessert we'd each eat one of those big old sugar-frosted Southern Cinnamon Rolls. Probably the same kind your daddy made whiskey with. Those things were big and they were cheap and they would solid fill you up.

"I guess ice was the main problem with eating out on the road. That was the one that threw us. See, we could never keep things cold enough to keep them long. You know like butter and bacon and milk. Later on we got smarter and picked up one of those old coolers and went over to the ice house and bought a couple fifty-pound blocks. I'd pack them down with sawdust and wrap them with croaker sacks or blankets, anything to keep them from melting so fast. But you get down south far enough, say Alabama or Mississippi, it didn't matter what you did, those blocks would go down faster than the Titanic.

He smiled, there was a joke coming. "You heard the one about the New York newspaper man talking to the 110-year old farmer named Jefferson down in Mississippi?"

"Nope, let's hear it."

"Well this reporter says 'Mister Jefferson'"—Satch was now sounding as if he'd been born and raised on Flatbush Avenue in Brooklyn—"'you've been around long enough to see the automobile invented, the airplane invented, the atom bomb invented, and a man hitting a golf ball up on the moon. I mean you have been here long enough to see some major changes in this world. Now what my paper and I'd like to know is what was the main discovery or invention that changed your life and that you are grateful for?'

"And old Jefferson thought about it and thought about it some more. Then he lit his pipe, sucked on it a little bit, and thought about it some more. Finally he looked around the room real slow like and began smiling. Then he raised his arm, real slow like, and pointed his pipe at the window and said, 'Screens.'

"Listen, I got another New York reporter story you got to hear. Be sure and remind me to tell it. OK? But right now let's get this show back on the road. Ask me something else."

I ran him by the old standard, if he had to do it all over again, what would he have done if he hadn't gone into baseball? He gave it a little thought but not too much.

"I wouldn't want to be no dentist. Now I got nothing wrong with dentists. God knows I've seen enough of them and they've done some wonderful work on me, but I'd just as soon be on the outside. Outside in the open. But I guess if I had my pick, if it wasn't baseball, I guess I would have liked to have done something in music. Maybe singing and dancing and cutting the fool up on stage. Maybe even writing music. I can still come up with brand-new tunes on my guitar, and when me and the boys get together we do some pretty fancy close harmony. Tell you something else I might have liked, managing a nightclub. You know working with the band and taking care of the people and seeing that everything moves along pretty smooth."

"How about managing a baseball team?"

"Hell, I gave up on that a long time ago. That's still a white man's job. It's too bad too because I could show every one of those pitchers out there a little something. Maybe if I'd been born about twenty years later I'd have had a crack at managing. Bo, I'm not complaining, let's keep that straight, I just came along too early."

He pointed his long finger at me. "You know why I like working with you?"

"Why's that?"

"Well the money's not too bad." He grinned. "But the main thing is you don't take any notes. Most reporters get all crouched in over their pads and are writing away while I'm yakking and, hell, I can't help it, I start trying to read what they're going to write. And when I see what they're putting down that's when I start clutching up. Weird, isn't it?"

"Naw, I don't think so. Lot of people don't like to be written about."

He asked me who all I'd interviewed and I rattled off a string of West Coast movie stars, singers, and guitar pickers. Satch said he knew almost every one of them. I told him I even had lunch one time with my all-time favorite prize fighter—Sugar Ray Robinson.

His eyes lit up and he whistled one long clear note. "Man, you know Sugar? That's my main man. He's the greatest. The goddamn greatest one out there."

He sat back proud of himself with his two fingers up in the air side by side. "Me and Sugar Ray, just like that. Used to run around Harlem together—we'd hit all the spots—Small's, the

Ebony, the Cotton Club, the Peppermint Lounge down on Fifty-something Street. Hell, I think we were there the night old Chubby Checker introduced the Twist. Sugar Ray had him a purple Cadillac, a convertible. That thing had fins that stuck up to your damn shoulders. And he had four or five women lined up all the time just to ride around in that boat. Oh man, we were great together. Hell, we'd get out on the dance floor and do little numbers. Once in a while Cab would come along. Now don't you know that had to be a threesome. And yeah, one time there we even drug old Bojangles along. I got some shots out at the house, they're all there. All four of us."

He smiled. "Now that Twist was one dance you could get ahold of by the neck and never turn loose. Hell, you could go as fast or as slow as you wanted. You could dance to that thing all night long."

I told him I'd heard that Sugar Ray had tried tap dancing and asked if he knew about that.

"Hell yeah. There ain't nothing I don't know about him. Sugar Ray, the greatest pound for pound boxer that ever put on a jock. Hell, I bet I saw a dozen of his fights. That fool would fight once a month if you let him. Remember when he lost to that bird Turpin? He got him a rematch that same month and beat him till he dropped. Man he was smooth and he was good and he was tough and he was cool. And I'll tell you something else he'd do, he'd get us some fine, fine seats, right up front.

"The last time I saw him was out in Hollywood when I was doing that movie with Robert Mitchum and Julie London. I met up with him in the commissary out at Twentieth Century. Listen to this, that guy is a salt freak. I mean it. He was eating corn beef hash with a couple eggs and I was sitting right in front of him. Here's what he does, he takes the saltshaker and starts shaking that thing until he's got every inch of that hash covered. I mean it looked like it had been snowed on. I said, 'Man that is one helluva lot of salt. That stuff will kill you quicker than a train. Why you want to do that to yourself?'

"And you know what he says? He says, 'Satch, I'm a salt

freak. Always have been and always will be. But I work it out doing roadwork. That's how I keep in shape.'

"And he was too, he was hard as a stone and he always looked top notch. I always figured being as good-looking as he was made him one helluva defensive fighter. See, he didn't want to get that pretty face all scarred up. See, he was saving that for his women. And don't you know he had them.

"Oh, I forgot something. On that opening night of his tap dancing at the Apollo, you know what that fool told the reporters?" Satch was laughing. "'At last I've found my true métier.' Ain't that funny? I can just seeing him saying that." With the tip of one finger, Satch raised his chin and in a high and overarticulated voice he reported, "'At last I've found my true métier.'

"He was doing some TV series out there but I can't put my finger on which one right now. But man, let me tell you something and you can put this down as gospel, that boy could box, what you talking about. He was a pure T-joy to watch. Best left there's ever been. And he could jab that thing at you so fast you didn't know where it was coming from. Hell, I did a little sparring with him one time. He just swarmed all over me and I don't think I laid a glove on him. Bo, right there's a good example of those fast and skinny legs I was telling you about. Maybe sometime I'll tell you the difference between a white woman and a black woman. But not right now."

He snapped his fingers, remembering something. "You ever get a chance you take you a good look at the film when he knocked out Gene Fullmer with that left jab. That thing didn't travel six inches but it lifted Fullmer right off the floor. Beautiful. Just beautiful. Yeah, no doubt about it, he was the best. The very best of the very best. In his prime no one could touch him. And like I said that fool would fight every other week. He couldn't get enough of it."

He talked for awhile about eating at the Twentieth Century commissary and about all the movie stars that had come over to his table to see him and how much he liked it out there.

Then he stopped. "Bo, listen here, I can talk about so damn many things it will make your head swim. Hell, that's one of my troubles, my motor mouth, I can't shut up. Let's just back up here and get back to your article. Now you got to be firmer, you got to tell me exactly what you want and you got to hold me to it. OK, now what you want me to talk about right now."

"You're doing fine. But right now I want to hear the New York reporter joke."

"Hey now, that's great. You'll love it because this is a really funny story. This hotshot New York Jew reporter was interviewing an old retired black field hand down in Mississippi and he says, 'Mister Jefferson,' or whatever his name was, 'I have been doing a considerable amount of research on what the American Negro wants. And I have come to my considered conclusion that what you and your people want is your rightful place in the sun.'

"Well old Jefferson sits back in his rocking chair packing his corncob and then real slow like, he starts shaking his head. 'No sir, that ain't it. That ain't it at all. Because you see, we have had that. We've had about all of that that we can stand.' Then he lit his pipe and took a long slow drag, 'What we'd like now is a little piece of that shade.'

I was laughing. "Now that's one I'm going to take back home."

Satch said, "Yeah I like that one too. OK, now let's get serious. Ask me something I can get with."

I said, "All right, I want you to try and fill me on what happened when you went up to Cleveland. Bill Veeck hired you, didn't he? Or was there someone else? And tell me about those first games, especially the ones against Chicago."

"Yeah there was someone else in there backing me up besides Veeck. Veeck was the main man but Abe Saperstein was my old ace in the hole. See, he was managing the Harlem Globetrotters. Like I told you I played in a few exhibition games with those boys. You know Goose Tatum and Meadowlark Lemon, tall old skinny cats like that. We had more fun than a barrel of monkeys. Anyhow, Bill Veeck was managing the Indians and they were fighting it out for the pennant with the Yankees and his bull pen was running low, so he asked Abe Saperstein to keep his eye peeled for a couple pitchers.

"Abe told Veeck I could fill the bill, and Veeck said, 'OK, let's give that old bag of bones a tryout.' Abe said he called me that but he was laughing when he said it.

"Anyhow Abe Saperstein called me and the tryout was all set.

"Man, I remember that phone call right now just as clear as clear. Me and Lahoma whooped and hollered and started dancing and we didn't stop until we danced through every room in the house and were out onto the porch. I'll tell you the music we danced to, Louis Prima and Keely Smith doing 'That Old Black Magic.' Great song. Great song. It gets wild and loose and you can really go with it. Hey, that's another Johnny Mercer tune. Yessiree, that's another Mercer song.

"Now this may seem hard to believe but it's as gospel as Matthew, Mark, Luke, and John. I got my Cleveland Indians tryout on the exact day of my birthday. July seventh. OK, that was 1948 and I'm exactly forty-two years old and I was so nervous and scared I was about to jump right out of my skin. See now, they were both there, the big men, Lou Boudreau and Bill Veeck, and they were there to check me out to see if I had any stuff left. Lord, I don't know when I'd been so scared.

"So Bill Veeck told Lou Boudreau to catch a few balls while I warmed up and then hit a few. Veeck said OK to that and I said OK to that too. Then Boudreau asked me if I wanted to warm up first and said I could take a lap around the park.

"He wanted me to run fifty yards and then walk fifty and then run fifty more until I'd gone all the way around. So I said OK and I started out. I guess I ran about ten or twenty yards and I told myself, no, this is never going to work. Nosir. So I ambled back and told them I'd just as soon not do too much running. I told them I didn't need too much of a warm-up. Now normally when I'm horsing around, I'll light a cigarette, like Charley told you, and take a couple drags and say that's all the warming up I need. But I didn't do that that day. Nosir. Like I said I was pretty damn nervous and I wasn't going to be wasting any juice screwing around like that. Not that day. Even though I'd already been pitching twenty-five years, and more than that, this was the big leagues. This was the Indians. The real Indians, the Cleveland Indians, and I was trying out for Bill Veeck and Lou Boudreau, men who knew baseball inside and outside. And they were there with only one thing to do. They were there to look me over. And pod-ner they did that, they looked me over.

"Anyhow, Lou Boudreau picked up a catcher's mitt and squatted down behind home plate and told me to go out to the mound and toss him a few. He said, 'OK, Satch, let's see what you got.'

"Well at first I tossed them in real easy like to make sure I was loose enough. Then after a few of those I began to put a little something on it. Not a lot, just a little. After about ten of these I began winging them in there pretty good. Nothing full-bore right then because see, I was still holding back something for when he picked up that bat. Now right in here, at this exact time, Lou Boudreau was leading the American League and the National League with a batting average of a flat four hundred. You can check that one out, a flat four hundred. If I'm lying, I'm dying. So, like I said, I'm saving up a little something because I had to be careful with a hitter like that. And another thing, I'd never faced this bird before and I needed a little time to watch what he was doing with his knees and figure him out.

"So Boudreau said, 'Well you look pretty good. But right now I'm going to hit a few.' So he hands the mitt to another guy and he picks up a bat and gets ready.

"About this time Veeck asked him if he wanted him to shag the balls and Boudreau said, 'Yeah but get out in right field. This guy's going to be hard to pull to left.' But Veeck decided not to go out in no outfield. What he was going to do was stand in behind the catcher and see how hard Boudreau was going to hit me.

"Boudreau was right, he sure as hell wasn't going to pull me because everything I gave him was on the outside corner. But now I was putting some heat on it and he started missing them. I gave him a couple Bee balls and one of the old Troubles and all he did was watch them go by. When I whipped in my old Stinger, I don't even think he saw it. Later on, Bill Veeck told me that after I began winging them in that I threw twenty pitches and nineteen were strikes. And all Lou did was hit one pop fly. Right after that was when he flipped the bat over to the dugout and told Veeck, 'Don't let him get away. We can use this one.'

"But see, I didn't hear this because I'm still standing out there on the mound sweating bullets and I don't know what in the hell's going on. Veeck told everyone later on that Boudreau was leading both leagues right then in hitting .400. But against old Satchel he was .000.

"But let me back up here. See, I'm still out there on the mound and didn't know if I was in or out. As far as I was concerned all they could be doing was trying to figure out what kind of ticket they had to buy me to get me back to Kansas City. See, you never know what managers like that are looking for or what they're seeing. So I'm still standing out there on the mound in that big old Cleveland stadium looking over all those empty seats and I'm sweating so hard it's running down my armpits and dripping from my nose, because I don't know what the hell's going on.

"Anyhow, while I'm out there Boudreau and Veeck were over by the dugout and they kept looking back at me and talking away. To this day I don't know what they said, but it must have been something pretty good because the next thing you know we're in the locker room and Boudreau is handing me an Indian uniform and telling me to try it on. Well it was long enough and it was skinny enough and it fit like casing on a hot dog. It was perfect. And let me tell you something, that uniform felt like nothing I'd ever worn in my life. It felt wonderful.

"And then right on top of that Bill Veeck put his arm around my shoulder and put the icing on the cake and said, 'Satch, you're fine right now. Just fine. But Lord, it's too bad you didn't come up to the majors with us in your prime. You'd have been one of the all-time greatest. Right up there with Feller and Dean. And I'll take a damn oath on that one.' That's exactly what he said, 'Satch, you'd have been one of the all-time greatest.'

"That Veeck was and still is one of the best managers out there. Now listen to what he did. First of all he gave Abe Saperstein fifteen thousand for finding me. Then when I told him how Mr. Wilkinson and Mr. Baird had sponsored me all that time in thirty-eight when my arm went dead, and I thought they should be getting a little something too. He said, they sure as hell do, and he gave them five thousand to split. Now there ain't many men out there that will do that. You know how much Mr. Branch Rickey gave them, I mean Wilkinson and Baird, when he took Jackie Robinson from the Monarchs? Take a guess? And don't forget, when they took Jackie out of the Monarch infield they left a big hole out on second base and a big hole in that batting lineup and you better believe it."

I said, "I'd pass on that one."

Satch said, "Not one Indian head copper penny. Bo, you got to realize managers ain't going to give you doodley-squat unless you spread their ass out over a barrel. That's the way it's always been. And that's why Bill Veeck is so damn special. And hell, I guess that's why I love old Burr-head." He smiled. "That's what Lou Boudreau always called him."

CHAPTER 11

SATCH WAS FEELING good thinking about Veeck and that first day with the Indians and I decided to take the plunge and try and get him talking about a couple low spots, when his arm went dead and he and his first wife Janet were breaking up. I asked if he wanted to talk about it.

He said, "Sure, let's do it. It's going to hurt but let's get it over with. Now where in the hell am I going to begin on all this? OK, I guess it all goes back to when I left Gus Greenlee's Pittsburgh Crawfords. You know to this day I don't know what in the hell Crawfords means, unless it means the old Crawford Grill. Anyhow, this was in thirty-six and I was making money hand over fist for him, pitching red-hot ball and didn't have a care in the world. Now right in here was the time when the boys were coming up from Cuba and the Dominican Republic with their pockets full of money to recruit ballplayers. A lot of people were calling them pirates, but hell all they were doing was exactly what every damn manager and team owner in the leagues had been doing every since they could walk. I mean they weren't any more pirates than you or me.

"But this gets kind of funny right in here because Gus and a couple more owners took a couple of these recruiters down to the magistrate and tried to get them fined and deported. Hell, they even tried to get them locked up. Well sir, you talking about a total catastrophe, this was it. Remember the movie *Zorba the Greek*? Anthony Quinn plays Zorba—now that's another one of my all-time favorites. Anyhow in the movie whenever things go wrong he says, 'total catastrophe!' And that's what this was, a total catastrophe. Because the minute old Gus opened his big mouth and tried to sue these Cubans everything backfired on him. What happened was the recruiters wound up telling the judge how they'd just hired one of our speedball pitchers—a guy named Ernest Carter—for a thousand dollars for a few weeks' work. And that's when the old shit hit the fan. Because back in thirty-six if you made twenty bucks a week you were in hog heaven. Anyhow, when the boys heard about money like that floating around, they stopped right there in their tracks and went looking for those two boys from the islands.

"Well a couple days after the hearing those recruiters came to see me and said they'd been sent up by President Rafael Trujillo who wanted the best pitcher in the United States, and they'd decided that that was me. Now let me clear this up. I had a good contract with Gus and the Crawfords and I wasn't about to jump down to some damn jungle unless I was sure they were talking about some really big money. So I just sat back and listened to their proposition. See, I've heard these offers before but most of them was all talk, most of them never came up with the old green stuff. But these boys from the islands did not screw around. Nosir. They came right to the point. They said they would give me thirty thousand dollars, all I had to do was get eight more players and they'd fly us down there and pay all the expenses. Back in thirty-six, thirty thousand sounded like thirty million. I figured I could give each player three thousand. That would be twenty-four thousand and I'd keep the six.

"I thought about it and I thought about it some more, then I asked him if I could see the money, and they said they would make the arrangements and we'd meet the next day. Now I'd been involved in a few deals like this where everything gets said and everything gets promised and we all shake hands and have a drink and then everything kind of evaporates and all you wind up doing is staring at the damn room and the phone bill in the morning. But this deal went through like it was greased. The next day they show up and they hand me a brand new bankbook, and there it was right on the top of page one, in black and white—he'd deposited thirty thousand in my account. So right away I'm rounding up the players and in no time we're down there in the islands with the rum and the senoritas and the mariachis and having a helluva time. So right in here old Gus is getting himself an even bigger headache. Because when the word spread of this kind of money floating around looking for a home, a bunch of boys from every team in the league began doing some fast signing up and traveling. I bet we wound up with half of Gus's team down there. We had all the best ones: Cool Papa Bell, Henry Williams, and even my old buddy Josh Gibson.

"Of course it wasn't all tacos and senoritas down there. Problem was Trujillo wanted a championship team so he could beat out his rival, this big strongman down there on the other side of the island, who had him a pretty good team too. So right up front they told us all we had to do was not lose. Well hell that didn't bother me because we had all the big hitters and I had my Bee ball going and all my moves. But then I started noticing the men guarding us were all carrying guns and long knives in their belts and had these long-ass straps of ammunition across their bellies. Man they looked mean. And they were mean. Hell, what you talking about, that gang of goons would stand out in the hall at night guarding us when we went to sleep. We never did find out if they were guarding us from the other team or they were guarding us to make sure we didn't bail out of there. So all this started getting me nervous as hell.

"Anyhow, we kept playing and we kept winning but then we came up on the championship series against Trujillo's big enemy, I forget his name now. And if I knew it I wouldn't be able to pronounce it. But man, he was mean too, and he had his own troops out there. Big hats, big moustaches, big guns, big old long knives, and all that extra ammunition. So here we are tied three games apiece and we're going into the biggest game down there with all these guns and knives around and hell every one of us was so scared we could hardly breathe. And to top all this off, just before the game they tell us that this was the game we had to win—*or else.* I mean the rumors started flying—about whoever wins the game wins the government, and whoever wins the game wins the island. And someone said something about a damn firing squad for the losers. Crazy, wild things like that. But with all those guns and shit out there we didn't know what to believe.

"Well that *or else* stuck in my craw and it stuck in a lot of our boys' craws, so while we were playing I'm telling you something, we were nervous. We couldn't hit; we couldn't field; and I was pitching like a registered moron—they were hitting everything I threw in there. And every time we looked over in the stands and saw all those troops, we got even more nervous.

"Anyhow by the seventh we were behind—five to four—and right in there you could see the swords flashing and those guys getting ready to come out on the field and cause some real trouble. Hell, it looked to me like they were getting ready to break out the black blindfolds and line our asses up against one of those old firing squad walls. See, you get that scared and you start imagining all kinds of things.

"Well right in there I started asking the good Lord to make my ball behave and let us get a couple runs. I figure he must have heard me, because right in then I shook something loose and my Bee ball began humming on the outside corner and I shut them down. Then we picked up two runs and we finally squeaked out of that. Lord, that was one nasty mess to be in. Nasty. Anyhow, we all went back to the hotel and had a meeting and decided we'd had enough of Mr. Rafael Trujillo and the whole damn Caribbean. I mean we liked that rum and we loved those senoritas and the music but that many guns and knives and all that extra ammunition were just too much for us to deal with. So the next day we were packed and out of there. We got on that plane in a hurry and right when we were taking off, right when that plane left the ground, I counted one, two, three and we all hollered out 'Adios amigos!'

"Funny how that old greenback talks, ain't it? See when we pulled out for the Dominican Republic for what we thought was going to be all that easy money, the club owners were raising hell, saying we were destroying baseball and ruining the Negro League. Well you know what I said to that, right to their faces, was you guys pay us a decent salary and no one would even be thinking about jumping to another team. But hell, that bunch would hold on to a dollar bill until old George screamed in pain. I mean it. That was one of the tightest bunch of bandits that ever walked; it was like they had fishhooks in their pockets.

"Anyhow, when we got back from down there those managers were so glad to see us they didn't say a word. Not word one, mind you. See, they knew they needed us to make them some money—and that's the goddamn long and the short on that one. If you're making money for someone then you got no problem with them. The problems come when the money gets tight. OK, so I'm back with a whole lot of publicity, which shoots me up in the marketplace. And right away I'm getting all these new brand offers; they were coming in from everywhere. And if it was a good deal I'd go for it. I'd say, 'I'll be there, send me a contract and send me some traveling money.' But see, and this is where that bunch was so stupid, they'd say, 'Come on out, we'll pay you when you get here.' And I'd say something like 'well let me think about it a little bit.'

"So while I'm thinking about it they're putting out advertising and announcing on the radio and to the newspapers that I've actually joined their club and they got me under a contract and I'm going to be there on such and such a day and I'm going to be pitching for them on such and such a day. See, everything they're saying is a damn lie. Anyhow, they'd keep calling me and saying, 'Now Satch, we're expecting you to be here on Monday or Tuesday or something.' And I'd say, 'I'll be there but you got to send me that traveling money, like I asked you.' And right here's where they made their big, big mistake with Satch, they said, 'No, you go on and pay that and we'll reimburse you when you get here.' So when I'm hearing this and I'm saying well let me think on that, in my head I'm saying something else, I'm saying, 'adios, compadres, you ain't getting no Satchel Paige like this. Not this time around you ain't!'

"Now catch this, right in here was when all those stories of me promising to play and breaking contracts and not showing up got started. Because those managers had to cover their ass with the press and explain how they had me contracted and how I swore I was going to be there. Hell, no one ever heard the other side of that story. My side of the story. But that's how those damn rumors started, and then every paper in the country picked it up and made it ten times worse. Like I said, once one of those stories get printed the other reporters just write it up again and make it a little saltier. And then to make it even better they'd write how they tried to reach me but I was unavailable for comment. Now Bo, you know yourself that's a lie because one thing I am always available for is a comment, no matter what it is. Am I right or am I wrong?"

"You're right, Satch."

"OK, I was still signed up with Gus Greenlee and I was on a good salary and everything was perking along pretty smooth. But then right in there, and I mean for no reason, things started falling apart between Janet and me. We were real close and real tight at first but with me being gone most of the time and her wanting to settle down, well things started getting raggedy out on the edge. Now don't get me wrong, she's a fine, fine woman, and we used to have us some times together. Lord that gal could dance. She could dance all night. But hell, so could I and for a long time there we really rang the old bell. But things happen between a man and a woman. Things you don't understand and, well, we just drifted apart. So when I got an offer to go pitch down in Mexico I said screw it and broke my contract with Gus and hightailed it south of the old border. I guess that was the wrong thing to do but I did it anyway and I stuck with it.

"So I played up and down Mexico and that is one helluva lot of territory. It's bigger than Texas and then some, and it's long too. Real long. Most people don't realize just how big and long that country is. And there's some great people down in there; seems like they're much more relaxed than we are and don't need all the front-end work we do. Maybe it's all those big hats and those siestas. They just get under that hat and lean back on a building and they go to sleep. Now that's something I got used to in a hurry. Siestas. Yessir, I love them. And I'll tell you something else they got down there, they've got some of the best guitar players in the world just hanging around the street corners. Seems like everyone plays something down there. Oh, and trumpets! Man, what you talking about, they play that thing like they invented it. I've never heard anything like it. It was sensational. It was beautiful. And the music down there is beautiful too. As a matter of fact I learned nine or ten of them songs on my guitar. When we get out to the house I'll play you a couple.

"Well a lot of my buddies from the Negro League were down there with me and we'd get together, and man, we had us some great times. The only drawback was the food. I never did get used to that hot stuff and those peppers and all those beans and things. It was good at first, real good and real different, but then after a while that stuff will tear you down. Anyhow, my stomach started acting up and right in there was when I started running into trouble with my doggone arm. I'm pretty sure I threw it out when I was throwing sidearm curves. I thought it was only temporary but then it got worse and before you knew it, I couldn't even lift it. Now you talk about someone scared, you are now looking at him. I was petrified, because I'd been counting on that arm ever since I was throwing rocks down in Mobile and playing at the Mount and right on up till right then. And listen to this, yeah, I forgot this little item, we weren't being paid no salary. I was paid for every game I pitched. So, if I didn't pitch I didn't get paid. And you know me by now, I hadn't saved dime one. Now you talk about being in a tight scrape down in old Mexico, it was me. So right in there was when that music down there went sour and didn't sound so good to me anymore. You know something, I never did find out what was wrong with my arm.. Never did. As a matter of fact when I came back to the States and went to a specialist, you know what that bird said, he said, 'Satch you will never pitch again.'"

I asked what year this happened. Satch said, "What year? 1938. Hell, here I am only thirty years old and I'm washed up. I'm over the hill. Here I am, no money, no job, no arm, and I'm two or three thousand miles from home. Yeah, and hell, I ain't even got no home. I sure as hell didn't have no wife. I guess I kind of thought of going back to Janet but that didn't make any sense. Hell, I figured if I couldn't hold on to her when I was on top of the heap, I sure as hell couldn't hold onto her when I was down on the bottom. And right then with all that working against me I was on the bottom. Hell, below that. I'd gotten to one bottom and there was another bottom down there just looking up at me, just waiting for me. Oh, I had my car and my other stuff like my clothes and shotguns and fishing tackle and all. But the main thing that held it all together was gone, my arm. And along with the arm I'd lost Janet. Man, that was a hard few months there, let me tell you. So I had to regroup and I had to do what I had to do. So, I started loading up the car and hitting the pawnshops. See, that's the only place I could raise any money."

I asked him, "No one wanted you? Satch, that's hard to believe."

"They wouldn't touch me with a ten-foot pole. I called them all too, and I told them I could play first base until my arm came back or I could coach or do anything just so long as I could get on their payroll. But they all said the same thing. Well, it sure as hell sounded like the same thing. All about, 'Satch you ran out on us in thirty-five,' or 'where were you in thirty six when we needed you?' And all about how tight money was and crap like that. No, they wouldn't even look at me. Bo, I'm telling you something here and you be sure and get it straight, that managing and club-owning crowd are some sorry-assed people. When you're down and out and you ask them for some help, all they're going to do is shove their hands in their pockets and turn their backs and walk on off. We used to have a little riddle about how the owners treated the players. Used to run, 'Guess what the elephants sang when they danced with the chickens? Every man for himself. Every man for himself.'

"Now I'm going to take everything back I said bad about the owners and the managers. Because it wasn't too much later that I got a call from J. L. Wilkinson and Tom Baird, those were the boys who owned the Kansas City Monarchs. Right off the bat they told me arm or no arm they'd bought my contract from Newark—see old Gus had sold it to them when I went to Mexico—and I had a job. All I had to do was show up.

"Of course there was a catch to it. I wasn't actually signing up with the Monarchs; I was signing up for the Monarchs' traveling team. I asked them if I wasn't good enough for the Monarchs why did they even bother signing me up at all. And Mr. Wilkinson said, 'Well Satch, we figure your name will draw in some fans, and well, we just thought you needed a hand right now.'

"Later on I found out that Wilkinson and Baird hired a lot of ballplayers who were down and out or in trouble. Wilkinson used to say us ballplayers had done a lot for the Negro League and they just wanted to pay us back.

"Well my luck was beginning to come back a little bit, because out on the road I had this great coach, Knut Joseph, and he did more for me than anyone in my life. See, he was convinced if I just kept taking it easy and working on that arm just a little bit at a time it was going to come around. But I wasn't. I figured I was all washed up and it was all long gone and over. But old Knut made me get out on the field and play first base just to get me out there. And every day he and I would toss the ball back and forth trying to get a little something going. But Lord, it was hurting so much I didn't know what I was doing. We kept at this for a few weeks, or maybe it was longer than that, and he told me he wanted me to pitch an inning just to get the feel of being out on the mound. Well, I went out there and I could barely get that ball over the plate much less put anything on it, and all the time it was hurting me like holy hell. I said I was coming in but Knut hollered out for me to stay out there. So I did, and I kept throwing stuff like Alley Oops and softball slow pitch underhands, anything to move that ball. Man it was painful, and it was embarrassing because everything I threw in there those boys were slapping right over the fence. And everything I threw made my arm sting so bad I had tears in my eyes.

"But Knut stuck with me and kept making me soak that arm in hot water, almost scalding, and that helped a little too. I tried pitching again and I still couldn't strike anyone out. All I was doing out there on the mound was going through the damn motions.

"Well, here's exactly what happened. We'd been on the road a month or so and I think we were up in Canada about this time. I hadn't thrown a thing in a few days and Knut said he wanted me to try pitching for another inning, just for the hell of it. So I went over on the sidelines to throw my warm-ups, and man I was dreading it. Now, here's the way it was with the warm-ups—that first pitch I threw would make it hurt so bad I'd want to drop to my knees. So, you talk about something being afraid, I was immortally afraid of that first one. But I was determined to do what Knut was wanting me to do. See, right in here old Knut was the only friend I had out there, and I figured I had to at least try and hold on to him.

"Anyhow, when I was standing on the sidelines getting ready to throw that first one, I was one scared hombre. Lord, I was afraid. Well I jiggled that ball a little bit and rolled it around trying to get up my nerve, then I said the hell with it and wound up and threw it. I didn't have doodley-squat on it, just an old lob the catcher had to pick up on the bounce. But then suddenly it hit me right between the eyes, there wasn't any pain. None! Not a damn bit! My arm felt pretty good. Not great, but pretty good. But the main thing was I wasn't in no pain. Lord, that felt good. Then I threw again, still real slow like. And this time there wasn't any pain again. Then one more time. Now right about now I'm laughing away like a kid because I'm so damn relieved I don't know what to do. Then I told the guy catching me I was going to throw a fastball. And that's exactly what I did. It wasn't anything special. No Bee ball. No Trouble ball. No Stinger. Just a little more motion and a little more speed but it was enough to know I was sliding over the hump. Next thing you know, here comes Knut rushing out to see what I was doing. And you talk about someone being happy. I kept throwing and I could feel the sweat popping. See I hadn't sweated in months because I hadn't been able to work hard enough to break a damn sweat, but now I was, and man did that old juice did feel good.

"When I finished up old Knut reached up—see he was a lot shorter than me—and put his arm around me like a father and when I looked down I swear if he wasn't crying real tears. And I'll tell you something else, but maybe you shouldn't be writing this up, I was crying too. Aw hell, go ahead and write it up, nothing wrong with people knowing a few things like that.

"That night Knut called Mr. Wilkinson and Mr. Baird and told them the news, and they said they wanted me to not rush it but to get myself back in shape. Then they said the sweetest thing I'd heard in a long, long time. 'Satch,' they said, 'we want you to join the real Monarchs for next year.'

"OK, now that was thirty-eight and the beginning of the thirty-nine season. Now during that time, while I was waiting for it to get started, I played everywhere I could, getting my arm back in shape. But the main thing I had going for me now was I was now playing for the Monarchs and I was not going to mess that up.

"Well sir, the thirty-nine and the forty season with me pitching for the Monarchs went by real smooth and my arm didn't give me a lick of trouble. Here I was thirty-two years old and I was pitching more and pitching better than I'd ever pitched. Listen to this one, and I bet no one in their right mind has done this one before. One day there I pitched in three games and won every one of them. If I'm lying, I'm dying. I mean it. See, Mr. Wilkinson was the man who invented night baseball and some days we'd be playing three games because people who worked all day could come out at night and see us play. And it meant a lot more money. Of course like I told you that night ball will cut you up because you never really get stoved up hot enough.

"But in thirty-nine I didn't care about anything but pitching as much as I could, as long as I could, so I could make sure my arm was going to be all right. And I did it pod-ner, I damn well did it.

"Anyhow, one day I pitched the morning game and I won that one. The deal was I'd rest the rest of the day and pitch the night one too. But during the second game we got into trouble, and I went in in relief in the sixth or seventh, and I won that one too. Then that night I pitched the whole game, nine full innings, and we won again. Now I guarantee there ain't nobody breathing or dead and buried in the graveyard that can come up to that mark."

He began laughing. "Hell, you know yourself there's pitchers out there, pitchers driving big Lincolns and Cadillacs and flying their own planes and grinning out from the backs of Wheaties boxes that don't win that many games in a whole season. Anyhow, all this is leading up to the fact that the next four years were my best. I had all my speed back, and my Bee ball or Trouble ball would go anywhere I told it to go. And control, what you talking about? Man, I could thread a needle in the night. They were saying I could nip the frosting off a cake or kill a mosquito out on that outside corner. On top of that I had my hesitation pitch, my sidearm, and my number one ace in the hole, my old Stinger. I had them all going, and I was as frisky as a teenager out there on the mound. Anyway I took the Monarchs to the Negro American League title in '39, '40, '41, and '42.

"That was four seasons back to back to back to back. And it sure as hell made Mr. Wilkinson and Mr. Baird and old Knut happy and made them some money too. But those three men deserved it because they were the only ones who had had any faith in me to get me through that bad period. So it was right then in those four years that I decided to settle down here in Kansas City because everyone here was treating me so good. I tell you, I was like a king around town. Everyone wanted to shake my hand or touch me or get my autograph or park my car or give me any kind of credit I wanted. Kids were lining up just to do my yard work. I mean people could not do enough for me. Hell, I even ran for mayor. Didn't make it, but I ran anyway. And it was right in here that I met Lahoma. You want to hear how I met with her?"

"Sure."

"Well, as you know, I've always been a camera fiend, I bet I got a million shots out at the house. Anyhow, one day I go to this drugstore and ask the girl behind the counter for some film. Well, right away I see that she doesn't know who I am, and like I said I was used to everyone knowing me, so right away I'm getting my damn nose out of joint. Don't ask me why, I just did. Then she tells me they don't have any film for my camera. So like some kind of registered fool I call the manager over and tell him the girl had been rude to me. Now the manager knows who I am so he says, 'Mr. Paige, if Miss Brown has been rude to you I'll fire her right this minute.'

Well I thought about it and I said, 'No, ain't no need to do that. All I want is the next time I come in she'll know how to conduct herself.' Man, now that right there was one of the dumbest things I'd ever said, and don't you think Lahoma didn't play that one back for me.

"Well anyhow, every day for the next four or five I showed up there. See, I was upset I'd caused her so much trouble and I wanted to smooth things out. And besides that, this Miss Lahoma Brown was a class-A-number-one looker, and I was trying to see if I could get her to go out with me. Well it took a while, yeah at least four or five or six more times, but I hung in there, and I finally eased in and broke her down and got her out. And right in there was when the romance began."

CHAPTER 12

"NOW LET ME tell you about playing for the Indians. You're going to like this because it's really wild. You see at first Lou Boudreau just used me in relief, and I was pretty good. But nothing terrific. See, I'm the kind of guy who likes to start a game and I like to finish it. I like for it to be my game from the minute that umpire brushes that plate off and hollers, 'Play ball.'"

Satch, Charley, and I were back in the Twilight Zone talking about his first games in the major leagues with the Indians.

"When I'm in relief, it just ain't the same. But anyway, I pitched pretty good but all I did was win one and lose one. Finally, it was the first week in August and we were right smack in the middle of the pennant race when Boudreau asked if I thought I could start. I told him I sure could and I was raring to go. So the next day here I am facing the Washington Senators right there in Cleveland in Municipal Stadium. What was nice was the papers announced I was starting and the fans filled the damn place. See, they were dying to see me and they poured into that stadium like water from a spigot. I think it was something over seventy thousand, which turned out to be the biggest crowd for a night game in Cleveland history."

Charley chipped in, "I was there; I saw that game. I didn't see an empty seat."

Satch continued, "I pitched pretty good for a first game; they hit me for only seven hits. I got six strikeouts and I only walked two. Not great, but good enough to win and that was all that mattered right then because I'd gotten over that big hump of my first start in the majors.

"Now during the Washington game we were in first place but New York, Philadelphia, and Boston were all breathing down our necks. It was really tight. So about a week went by and Boudreau didn't use me for nothing. All I did was just sit there. And that's one thing I don't like doing, I don't like doing nothing. But then when we dropped out of first and we were going to Chicago he asked me if I'd like to start. I said, 'Man yeah, that's my town. I'd love to start there. I'll make some phone calls and get some of my buddies out.'

"Well sir, that was a night to remember. First of all not only was old Comiskey Park packed, they had something like ten thousand out in the parking lot listening to the game on the radio. See, that's how loyal that crowd was to me. And listen to this, another four or five thousand was in there standing in the hallways and behind the posts and the supports where they couldn't even see the field. I mean it, they just wanted to be there. Someone told me he saw a man carrying a sign that read, 'Satch, we can't see you. But we're here anyway.' Now ain't that terrific?"

Charley said, "He's right, Bo, that's the way I heard it."

Satch went on, "That was one game I didn't let anyone down, the crowd, Bill Veeck, Lou Boudreau, and yours truly, me. I pitched that whole game, my first complete game, and it was a shutout, five to nothing. Hell, what you talking about, that White Sox crowd gave me a standing ovation for five or six or seven full minutes. Man, now that was something else. Bill Veeck said he'd never seen anything like it in his whole life.

"Then about a week later I got to face that same team, Chicago, again. But this time it was back in Cleveland. So know

117

◇

SATCHEL PAIGE'S AMERICA

what I did? I shut them out again. And the crowd that night was 78,382 paid attendance, which broke the record I'd already set against Washington. Not bad for an old spring chicken with bad teeth and living on soft foods. Right? And man, don't you know I remember that figure.

"Anyhow, like old Dizzy says, I was keeping on with the keeping on and we won that pennant. And a lot of reporters were saying that the six games I won for them, especially those shutouts, was the big difference."

We had another round and told a few jokes. Even Charley told one. When the jokes ran down I got back on track by asking Satch how he got in the habit of walking so slow when he went out to the mound and doing everything so slow.

Satch smiled at Charley and shook his head. "OK, that's a sneaky one, but let me see if I can handle it. See, Bo, when you're as tall as I am, six feet three and a quarter, there ain't many people out there that you're going to be looking up to. Most of them you're looking down on. So what I do by moving so slow and holding my head just so is I make them think I'm up there around seven feet. And when I get out on that mound I'm looking even taller than that. See, you got to realize a fastball pitcher has to be tall because he needs all that extra wingspan to get the leverage and motion he needs to move that ball the way he does. And don't forget this, that's all I am, a fastball pitcher.

"And another thing, baseball is like poker. You've got to be able to read people. Say the other team's new pitcher comes out of the bull pen and he's walking fast and rubbing the ball in his glove fast like and he's chomping away on his gum. Hell, it doesn't take a genius to know right off the bat that this bird's so nervous he can hardly breathe. Then he throws five or six warm-up balls and next thing you know he's mopping the sweat down. Hell, this guy's goose is cooked before he throws the first ball. Now that right there is something coaches ought to be teaching. They should be teaching you how to come out of the bull pen looking smooth and relaxed and how to keep the other team in the dark about what you got on your mind.

"Now you take me, that's one thing I know, and that's how to walk out to the mound. I read someplace where they were saying I looked like a Watusi chief when I'm walking out there, and hell, I liked that. Because I guess that's exactly what I'm trying to look like. I mean that's a great look, looking like a tall old chief standing on one leg out on the plains and looking things over, things like giraffes and elephants and operations like that. Now there ain't no way in the world somebody's going to be reading what's on a bird like that's mind. And it's the same exact thing with me. I mean you take a good long look at me out there on that mound with my long legs and long arms and big feet and my poker face and doing everything in slow slow motion, there's no way on this earth you're going to figure out what's on my mind. I could be thinking about pork chops or what was going on in Leningrad, Russia. I could be driving a Rolls Royce or riding a damn mule. See, I'm not giving anything away. I'm making them think. And that's something a batter shouldn't be doing. Thinking. Because once I get them to thinking, then I can move them over to worrying. And that's right where I want them. I want them worrying, because that's when I can break them down.

"And there's another little trick here; the black man has a big edge over a white man. You can't read a black man's face. No one can, not even another black. It's impossible. But with a white it's all there, wide open just like a newspaper. Bo, I'll tell you the truth on that one, I'd rather pitch to two or three whites than face one good black man any day of the week. Any day of the week and twice on Sunday."

Satch said he was tired of talking baseball. He had remembered something about the medicine shows and wanted to talk about that.

I said, "Fine with me. Let's hear it."

"Well, Bo, a lot of those medicine pitchmen had some moves besides pitching medicine. Hell, I guess if you can sell that stuff you can sell anything. But you take old Bartok, Milton Bartok, he could do anything. I mean anything. When the government started sending lawyers around to check on what he was claiming his medicine could do he'd wrap them right around his little finger and get them so confused they didn't know their ass from their elbow.

"He'd say his medicine didn't cure anything. He'd say nature cures everything, his stuff just helped it out a little. See, when he said that there was nothing those legal eagles could nail him on. And they never did get him. He was slick. Slick. I guess the reason he got out of the business was television was coming along and he could tell which way the wind was going to be blowing. So what he did was he sold his props and bought the Hunt Brothers Circus. I mean it, lions, tigers, elephants, the high-wire acts, the sideshows, the whole damn thing. One month he was up on stage doing Mister Interlocutor and selling medicine and the next he was out in the middle ring announcing the circus. That's the kind of guy he was. And if you don't think that takes some high-powered talent and some heavy-duty nerve, you better back on off.

"But, now listen to this, there were men and women out there that were a lot slicker than Bartok. But on top of being slick they were as crooked as snakes. I mean it. And that's the bunch that went into preaching, the biggest hustle there ever was. And hell, they're still out there raking in the money hand over fist."

He laughed. "See, you take a medicine show with all their trucks and canvas and their big crews, they had what you call a tough expense nut to crack. And they had to carry all those bottles and caps and labels and they had to have a place to mix that crap and store it. And the crowd that worked for them had to be paid on time or else they'd bail out on your ass. Because a lot of them were lowlifes. Bartok said he had a man working for him that was wanted in twenty-two states and he had to plan his year like he was moving over a damn checkerboard. See, that's the kind of trash they had to deal with.

"But the evangelists figured out a way to get rid of everything and almost everybody. They streamlined that show down to the bone, because all they needed was a skeleton crew to put up the chairs for the service and then put them back in the trucks when it was over.

"Hell, Oral Roberts even had a way of getting around that one. He'd tell his crowd that he was a poor preacher from Oklahoma or Arkansas, or wherever he was from, and he couldn't afford a crew for the chairs. So he asked them if they would help him get the seats out of the trucks for him. And they did it in a minute. I bet he didn't have five people on his staff when he started out."

I had to interrupt with an Oral Roberts story of my own. I told him he'd come to Columbia when I was thirteen and I'd gotten in the healing line to show off for my buddies. What I did was tell the ushers I had a bad stomach, so they let me in the line and we started moving up toward the stage. What happened was the closer I got the scareder I got. When I finally got up there I was shaking like a leaf and I knew he was seeing right through me. And he was. Because the next thing I knew he was holding my head and twisting my damn ear. I wasn't up there more than five seconds.

Satch sat back grinning. "Bo, that's pretty good. Pretty damn good. Too bad he didn't make you take off your shoes and walk across that rug in front of him. See, he's got these little copper wires running through it and he's got a man behind the curtain with a souped-up battery. They use it for people who can't hear. Now what they do is old Oral will burr his little finger way down in that ear and get that wax loose. Now just as he makes that ear pop, that guy backstage hits you with about twenty volts. I'm telling you, I've seen this one; most of the time those monkeys are jumping off that stage saying they can hear dogs barking in the next county."

He smiled and popped his hands together. "Hey, I got one that will knock you down. This guy Montgomery pulled it, and I saw it with my own eyes down in Shreveport. Now that boy had sass and he had spunk and that son of a bitch would do anything to make a buck. He called himself 'Montgomery the Magnificent,' so we aren't talking about a helluva lot of modesty here. Anyhow he was as tall as me but he had big arms and a big chest, hell, he was big all over. He'd been in the 'painless dentistry' business. What they'd do in that hustle was you grab your patient around the neck and squeeze so tight they don't even feel the tooth coming out. No lie, that's how that crowd worked. You check that one out. Those boys were strong, and they'd kill you for a dollar.

"Anyhow, Montgomery was the master of what they called the 'lizard switch.' And it was a beaut. Here's how it works. Now the evangelist has to be pretty good to pull this off but that's what I've been trying to tell you: a lot of these boys had fast hands and a set of nerves like jumper cables and balls as big as coconuts. Man they could do anything.

"OK, here's the hustle. Montgomery handpicks him some looper from the crowd who ain't too bright and ain't too strong and he brings him up on stage and starts working on him. What he does is pray over him, and as he's praying he's rubbing his hands up and down his arms, and up and down his legs, and up and down his back. Slow, real slow like. Now while he's doing this he's praying to Jesus to help him out and keep him on the right path.

"Then he'll start rubbing and praying a little bit faster and getting excited and before you know it he's telling the audience that he's pretty sure this old boy has a demon in him. He can feel it running around and if they'll pray along with him, he might be able to find it and get rid of it. Now right about this time is when he asks everyone in the tent to get down on their knees and pray with him so they can pray that demon out of this guy.

"So there's your setup, the victim's been hearing all this demon stuff and he's getting so scared his teeth are rattling and he can hardly stand up. All he wants right then is to be off that stage. But like I said, he ain't too strong and Montgomery has clamped down on his ass and no one's going to be getting away from him, especially in front of a big crowd like this. OK, so everyone in the crowd is down on their knees saying 'Sweet Jesus. Sweet Jesus. Sweet Jesus.'

"See, they're on a roll, and before you know it they've got that old tent rocking. OK, all of a sudden Montgomery starts shouting that he's found the demon and it's right between this guy's shoulder blades. Of course right then is when the looper starts really going crazy and whipping around trying to break loose but Montgomery has him in a damn death grip and he ain't going nowhere.

"OK, so right in here is where Montgomery makes his move. He reaches in his pocket and palms out about a six-inch lizard. Now before the show he's put about an inch of finger nail polish on the inside of one of his fingers and he's dusted it with a little ground glass—that's the way cardsharks used to mark their cards. Well now this next move is fast. I mean fast. He rakes that lizard's ass right over that glass, slaps the guy's shoulder hard, pow, and turns that lizard loose. Well sir, that lizard, with his ass on fire, jumps a couple feet, probably does a double backflip, and tears the hell out of there. What you talking about, that animal is flying. The congregation sees it. Montgomery points at it and screams out, 'The demon! That's him! Right there! We got the demon out of this blessed boy's back. He's cured! He's cured! He's as healthy as any y'all out there in this here room! Thank you, Jesus! Thank you! Thank you! Thank you, Jesus!'

"He starts dragging this guy up and down the platform so everyone can see him. Now while he's walking up and down and thanking Jesus, he gives his little three-piece band the high sign to play a little hype-up happy kind of hymn, and he and the guy and a couple sidemen come down with their buckets and go out in the crowd just a-smiling away and take up this big collection they've been waiting on. They call it the 'Hallelujah Offering.' And that's where the ten- and twenty-dollar bills start rolling in."

Satch smiled. "Now if that ain't smooth, hell ain't hot. And boy, don't you know that if a guy like 'Montgomery the Magnificent' don't know how to make money nobody can. You ever see Reverend Ike on TV?

"He's slick too. As slick as they come. Bet you never heard of A. A. Allen out of Tulsa?"

"No, don't believe so. What did he do?"

"More like what didn't he do. Son of a bitch turned out to be a raving alcoholic plus an A-number-one stone-looper crazy. Right there at the end he went completely crazy and started having fits and foaming at the mouth up on stage. He was claiming he could raise the dead. And listen to this, those poor saps out there were believing it and showing up with bodies. Now ain't that a bitch? Ain't that a bitch and a half? Right about then was when the police and the board of health authorities stepped in and put his ass away.

"Yeah some of those evangelists make the old medicine show operators look like a Boy Scout. Sad part is they come into town and take the clothes right off the line. They don't leave anything behind. At least with the old medicine show you had you a bottle of something with some alcohol in it and maybe some hard candy or an ashtray or something you could hold in your hand. But when this hellfire-and-damnation crowd left all you're going home with is your fists in your pockets because they ain't going to leave town until they've taken every red cent rolling."

Satch pointed at my beer. "Come on, drink up, I'm going to take you out to the house." He smiled. "Maybe one of these days we'll get around to talking some baseball."

SATCH'S HOME OUT on Twenty-sixth Street in Kansas City is a big, dark, two-story brick and frame with high ceilings and a heavy staircase leading up to the second floor. A small dining room on the ground floor is all baseball, filled with shelves of trophies, red-, white-, and blue-ribboned medals and awards, and gold-bordered testimonials of Satch's records. The walls are covered with photos of him clowning around with everyone from Wallace Beery to Julie London, from Bojangles to John Henry Lewis, the former light heavyweight champion of the world. "Great guy here. One of the best. Gus Greenlee was managing him back in Pittsburgh when he went to the top. You beginning to see how all this stuff starts connecting up? See what I've been telling you. Back then everybody knew everybody.

"Now right here's the boy that cured me of thinking I could go a couple rounds with anyone. See, for a while there I thought I was his sparring partner. No lie, I'd get in there and we'd go a couple rounds and I'd be bip bip bipping him and I thought I was king of the hill. But then it happened, one time I was bouncing up and down and feeling my oats and I caught him when he wasn't looking. Pow! I mean I stung him, right on the jaw. Next thing you know the lights were out and I was flat on my back on the floor looking up. Gus told me the first thing I said was, 'I stung him. Get me Joe Louis, I'm ready for him.'

"But Gus was so mad he hit the damn ceiling and cussed John Henry up one side of the wall and down the other. See right in there was when I was making all that money. Hell, I was probably the meal ticket for both of them."

Lahoma, his wife, called and we followed her out to the backyard and looked up at a big elm tree whose branches were scraping against the windows on the second floor. Lahoma, a good-looking woman who works as a pastry cook over the river in Kansas City, Kansas, was pointing. "You're just going to have to do something about this. The next high wind we get and we're going to have all kinds of bills."

Satch lit a cigarette and shook the match out. "I got some buddies down at the fire department. They said they were going to help me out on this."

Lahoma, who has a calm and steady voice, had heard this before. "That was last month; look how much it's grown since then."

"OK, I'll get with it. If they can't get here by Friday I'll do it myself."

Rita Jean, their four-year-old daughter, ran out of the house, jumped the steps, and began pulling on one of Satch's pockets. "Daddy, can I have a dime for the ice cream man? He's going to be here real soon. I can hear the bell."

"OK, darling." He gave her a dime and two nickels. "And get one for your mama, one of those strawberries she likes. OK, Lahoma?"

"Thanks, I'll go with her."

There are two kitchens in the house on Twenty-sixth Street; one upstairs, one downstairs. Satch explained that he likes to cook and he likes to do it by himself. "I don't do it all the time because Lahoma is the greatest cook and baker in the world. She can make a biscuit that's as tender as pound cake and so light that thing will float right off the table. But every now and then I'll get a craving for one of my old road meals. You know something like that hamburger and beans thing I was telling you about, and I'll whip it up. But most of the time I'm eating anything she puts out on the table. Anything. The Lord never made a finer cook than my Lahoma."

Later we went upstairs to one of the bedrooms where he unlocked a steamer trunk filled with clippings, posters, old gloves, and autographed balls. He laid the heavy lid back. "Well it's all here. To tell you the truth I just don't like looking through the damn stuff. It brings back too many memories. But you go ahead, take your time. Take all the time you want."

I went through a foot-high stack of photos showing him with movies stars, governors, prizefighters, club owners, and at least two hundred ballplayers. The old poster was near the top. Red on white with black trim:

KANSAS CITY MONARCHS
FEATURING THE WORLD'S GREATEST PITCHER
LEROY "SATCHEL" PAIGE
GUARANTEED TO STRIKE OUT NINE MEN IN THE FIRST THREE
INNINGS OR YOUR MONEY BACK.

There were photographs of him in his hunting clothes with his shotgun and his dog in his lap. Another of him in Durango, Mexico, shooting *The Wonderful Country*, where he played a cavalry sergeant. In one shot he's looking long legged and awkward on a horse. In another he's between the stars Robert Mitchum and Julie London, and in another, still on location in Durango, with Lahoma and their daughters Shirley Long and Lulu Ouida Paige.

There were still others of him clowning around at bat, shuffling in slow motion across the field heading for the mound, and one of him in the St. Louis Browns' bull pen stretched out on a La-Z-Boy recliner, with a canopy on top to keep the sun off, waiting to go in in relief. There was also an old eight-by-ten mounted in a black cardboard frame of a New Orleans team called the Armstrongs. And there at the side, dressed to the nines with two-toned shoes, deep pleated pants, and a floppy high-style white hat and grinning away, with an even dozen teeth flashing, was Louis "Satchmo" Armstrong.

I asked about it and Satch said, "Yeah, Louis had his own team back then. Pretty good too. The New Orleans Armstrongs. Man, that fool loved baseball and he loved to put on a show. Hell, he'd get Lena Horne to come out to the games and toss in the first ball. Now, as far as I'm concerned, that's the most beautiful woman in this world. Maybe they got something finer in the next one, but she's number one down here. Now I know I got plenty of shots of her around here someplace. But Louis and I rambled around a little bit too and hit the clubs. Couple times it was Louis and Cab Calloway and me. Now don't you know we had to look like something else. Yeah, those were some tall times in New Orleans back then."

He spread photographs out on the coffee table and began pointing out Josh Gibson and Poindexter Williams and "Double Duty" Radcliffe, one of his old catchers, and one of Cool Papa Bell doing a comic swan dive into second base. There were other members of the Monarchs, the Black Barons, and the Crawfords that he'd forgotten. But he knew most of them. Some were hanging out of the Satchel Paige All-Stars bus; others were climbing the ramp to the Satchel Paige DC-3 that he toured Mexico in; and others were simply lazing around the dugout waiting for a game to start. Everyone was dressed and grinning in the nightclub shots and the roll call ran: Cab Calloway, Sugar Ray Robinson, Bojangles, John Henry Lewis, Lena Horne, Wallace Beery, Martha Raye, and Mickey Rooney. Satch even had old brown and out-of-focus shots of the medicine shows.

But one particular shot caught my attention and held it. It was a long, narrow shot framed in mica-flecked black cardboard showing a group of medicine show owners at a railroad station—across the top it read "New Orleans, 1930." Satch said he had no idea who they were or how he got it. But there they were at the platform, posing stylishly beside their steamer trunks of costumes and medicine. The women were wearing high-collared long coats that swept the floor and fruit- and bird- and flower-decked hats. The men, in three-piece suits and spats on their shoes, were looking extremely pleased with themselves as they held big cigars out at sophisticated angles. They could have held the pose for ten seconds, thirty seconds, or a full two minutes if they had to. Somehow, as they stood there in the slanting sun in front of the long-gone City of New Orleans, the cameraman had caught it all, that fragile mixture of sly cunning and innocence reserved for skinny kids you see at the border selling Chiclets and their sisters. Satch smiled, "Bo, those were simpler times back then, simpler. People hadn't been exposed to so much and they trusted everyone." Then he added, "Even strangers.

"Listen here, I've got to run over to the drugstore and pick up a couple things. Stay here and make yourself at home. OK?"

"Fine with me."

After Satch left, Lahoma came upstairs with two glasses of iced tea, one for her, one for me, and sat on the coffee table. She asked if there was anything she could help me with. I wanted to ask what she thought of Satch going out barnstorming again but I didn't know how to ask the question. But she must have sensed something, because she said, "I guess he's telling you he's going out on the road again."

I weaseled around on that one. "Well yes, he has mentioned something like that."

"No, he's done more than any just mentioning it. Well, all I'm going to say about that is you make sure he goes before you go writing about it. I just don't want something like that coming out in the papers and then him not doing it. And now, I'm not going to say another word about any of it."

Lahoma went back downstairs and I kept going through the old clippings and old autographed balls. Then I discovered a series of eight shots of Satch pitching that were in sequence and I laid them out side by side by side and took a long hard look. What was surprising—why surprising I don't know—was his incredible hip rotation and high leg action and the enormous, seamless arcs of his arms. What was fascinating was the concentration and command in the set of his jaw and in his bright and glistening eyes. But what was so perfect—it was almost beatific—was in the last shot, after a strike had been called, and he was leaning in with both hands on his knees with nothing less than a pure and seismic satisfaction and pleasure shining in his face.

◆

After Satch came back from the drugstore he opened a closet and began pulling uniforms out and tossing them across the bed. "I got to find something I can load old Charley's big ass up in."

He held up a white blouse with black trim and Satchel Paige's All-Stars in red across the front, shook it and tossed it over a chair. "That ought to fit."

He began flipping through a stack of pants. "Take a guess at his waist."

I said, "Thirty-six."

"Thirty-six? Hell, I'm a thirty-four. He's got to be forty."

He found a forty and laid it on the blouse. "What I do is give each player two sets. That way when one gets dirty they can get it cleaned or if they can't find a cleaners they can wash it themselves. Not the greatest way to travel but that's the best we can do."

He had a notebook of players' names and sizes, and after matching them to the uniforms he stacked them up and began counting out socks. "Each player gets four pairs and two caps." He snapped his fingers. "Hold it, dammit, I forgot to ask Charley if he had shoes. You be sure and remind me on that. OK?"

"OK, you're sure he's coming along?"

"I hope to hell he does. I've got to have a catcher. But I'm not going to count on it until I see him in the wagon and we're on our way. Every year I get a guy like this. All they can talk about it going, going, going. Then when it comes time to get going, they get going all right. Going in the other direction. Well, we'll see tomorrow."

After the clothes were stacked we carried them down to the station wagon and loaded them up. Then we slid in the Coleman stove, the pots and pans, and two big cardboard boxes of cooking ingredients and canned goods. Despite what Lahoma and Charley said, it looked like this was the year Satch was going to get back out on the road. And it looked like tomorrow was going to be the day.

THE NEXT DAY the sky was clear, the temperature cool, and a breeze strong enough to push a paper cup across the road was coming in from the west. Around six, with the wagon loaded down with uniforms and supplies, we were riding out to the park to meet the team and Charley. "Satch. I got a question."

He was happy. "Lay it on me, Bo."

"After playing all that time against the Negro League and the majors wasn't it hard to get up to speed against a hometown team? You know what I mean?"

"Sure I know what you mean. And like everybody else you're dead wrong. As far as these rinky-dink teams are concerned we're like the New York Yankees. Those kids will be playing like there's no tomorrow. See, we're still the team everyone wants to beat. And I'm still the pitcher they want to hit. Hell, once in a while I'll let them all hit me. All nine of them, just so they can say they did it. I'll even let the batboy hit me."

We pulled into the parking area and Satch got out looking around. Down in one corner of the park, under a shade tree, the American Legion boys were stretched out on the grass under a big oak waiting. But Satch was looking for Charley and he was looking worried. "Now don't tell me he's going to be late. I don't want to be driving in the dark unless I have to."

As he strolled over to the tree with his hands in his pockets the boys got up and began tossing a ball back and forth. Satch raised his hands as if stopping traffic. "Hold it. Hold it. Y'all don't have to do that for my benefit. Go on, lie back down and take it easy. You'll get all the pepper you want tomorrow." He kept looking around. "Any of y'all seen Charley and Clete?"

The boys shook their heads and shrugged their shoulders.

Satch kept watching the parking lot. "Well, keep your eyes peeled. I want to get this show on the road as soon as we can."

It was over an hour later and Charley was still missing and Satch was pacing up and down, getting madder and madder. "That son of a bitch had my number. He could have told me this." He cut his eyes at me. "You still saying he's going to make it?"

"Yeah, he swore up and down he'd be here. Something must have come up."

"Yeah, I bet." He spat on the ground. "If he doesn't show I don't know what in the hell I'm going to do for a catcher."

By this time two of the boys were reading comic books, one was sleeping with his glove over his eyes, and the other two were flipping a ball back and forth. Satch hollered over, "Any y'all ever do any catching?"

Nathan spun the ball off the tips of his fingers. "Nope, not me."

Satch pointed at the kid sleeping. "How about Bobby, there?"

"Double nope. That's the only spot he's afraid of."

Satch said, "I don't blame him."

At 7:40, just as it was getting dark, Charley pulled his car into the end of the lot, with Clete in the backseat and someone else, that I couldn't make out, in the front. He was driving slow and seemed to be parking as far away from us as he could get. It didn't look good.

Satch started for the car in a hurry. When I trotted over to join him he waved me off. "No, Bo, I better do this by myself. I'm getting a bad feeling on this one."

Then I saw the problem. Charley's wife was in the front seat and even in the fading light I could see that the set in her jaw was saying it all. "Charley Martin has other things to do besides going helling-off on a road trip to god knows where with Leroy Satchel Paige."

I couldn't hear them talking but most of it was between Satch and Charley's wife. All I heard from Charley was his high-pitched "I understand! Dammit, I understand!" He never did get out of the car.

Satch came storming back pounding his fist in his hand. He was furious. He didn't know what to do with himself. Then he spun around violently and headed back to the car. They talked awhile, then Clete climbed out and followed him back to the diamond. Satch touched Bobby, the kid who was sleeping, with his toe and told him to go out to second base. Then, taking the ball from Eric and Nathan and a glove from Herman, he went out to the mound and began tossing in soft warm-ups to Clete.

Satch rubbed the ball in his glove and raised his voice to Bobby out on second. "Get behind the bag. Yeah, that's it. Set up for a pitch out."

Then to Clete. "OK, get that mitt out a little. That's it. Now a little lower. Perfect. Now keep it there."

Clete held his mitt waist high. "OK, Satch."

Satch looked in, "All right now, I'm going to hit it so don't go moving around. I want to see how fast you get it down to Bobby. Got it?"

"Yessir, I got it."

The ball came in with what looked like three-quarters speed right into the mitt. Clete with two quick smooth moves and still in his crouch whipped it down to Bobby, on the right side of the bag, exactly where Satch wanted it.

Satch nodded but didn't say anything. He tried again, and again Clete whipped it down on the right side low, right where a base runner would be sliding. Satch still didn't say anything. On the next pitch Satch put a little heat on the ball and it popped into the mitt like a firecracker. Clete was ready and set for it, and once more he burned it down to Bobby.

Satch finally spoke. "Not too bad. Not bad at all." Then he

grinned and popped his fist in his glove. "Hell, that's pretty dog-gone good." He turned and hollered down to Bobby, "How'd they look to you?"

"Perfect Satch. Perfect. No one's going to steal on that arm."

Satch rubbed his fist in his glove. "That's what I'm figuring. OK, Clete, now you got a job to do. Get over there and talk to your folks. If they say you can go, you're my catcher."

Clete leaped in the air, and hollering all the way across the diamond, flew back to the car. "Mom. Dad! Mom! Dad! You hear what Satch said. Can I? Can I? Please! Please! Please?"

Charley's wife started to speak but now Charley was the one doing the talking. I don't know how they worked it out but five minutes later Clete came racing back to the diamond with his eyes shining. "I can go. They said I could go. Man, this is really something." He was carrying Charley's spikes.

Satch walked back over to the car to reassure Charley and his wife that he would take good care of Clete, that he would write every other day and phone every other day. Then after Charley gave Clete some money and his mother kissed him and gave him a hug he trotted over and joined the others sitting under the tree.

◆

With the boys riding in their beat-up old Chevrolet and Satch and me in the station wagon we drove about a mile down the road to a Kentucky Fried Chicken. Satch said, "I better feed them now while I can."

We all went inside and after Satch bought everyone a four-piece dinner with cole slaw, mashed potatoes, three-bean salad, and two pints of milk, we filed outside and sat at the picnic tables facing the road. Satch was watching them eat. "Normally I'll take them to an all-you-can-eat place but tonight I figure it's special."

I said, "It sure is for Clete. I've never seen a kid so happy."

"Hell, they all are. I sure wish you were coming along, you wouldn't believe the brand of ball these kids can kick up." He paused. "Bo, tell you what you can do for me right now."

"Name it."

"If it's all right with you, I'd like to take the rest of that money now."

I pulled it out. "You're going to need it feeding this bunch."

Satch began creasing a twenty-dollar bill down the middle as he called Clete and he came racing over. Satch held the bill in his long fingers, then he sailed it across the table. "Here, go back in there and buy them some ice cream and some kind of cake or something. And hey, check that machine in the lobby. I think they got some fried pies. Get me a couple apples if they got it, but anything else is OK, too."

"OK, Satch."

As Clete rushed for the door Satch shouted, "Clete!"

He skidded to a stop. "Yessir."

"Quit all that damn running. And don't be so damn eager. Slow it down. Slow it down, save your strength."

"Yessir, Satch."

Satch shook his head. "And forget the sir. All I want you to do is take good care of that arm. We're going to need it behind the plate."

It was later; it was dark, and an orange red moon was rising down the road in front of us. "Bo." He waited for me to answer.

"Yeah, Satch."

He framed his hands in a director's square and aimed it at the moon. "There you have it, the prettiest thing in the whole damn world. Bo, right there is your basic southern moon and any time I'm heading into it I know I'm doing the right thing."

I guess I felt it before I heard it; he was sliding into a pitch.

"All I want you to do is take a long hard look at that beauty and then tell me you don't want to be out there with us."

The reds and oranges were running together and the rim was backlit in yellow gold: it seemed to be rolling up the road toward us. Satch's hand clamped on my arm and he began talking about the games and the crowds and the great nights that lay out there behind it. "Bo, you could have the time of your life out there. There ain't nothing like it. I mean nothing."

He was into the old medicine show pitch and was believing every word he said. "See, this may be my last time out. You know what that means? Hell, I'll probably come back and hang up my glove and my spikes and say OK I'm all through. I can't do it anymore. Reach over there and slide me that rocking chair. But Bo, you would have been there with me for that last barnstorm. My last everything. You'd be able to live it and write it and I'll be telling you more crap than you can jam into nine or ten books. Bo, I'm telling you something here. I'm telling you to make a couple phone calls and cut a few cords and come on out there with us. I swear to God, it's going to be something you'll never ever forget. All we're going to do is play ball and have fun. That's all we're going to do."

The moon lifted off the road and I could feel its tidal pull drawing me closer. His grip tightened, it seemed to be tingling. "Come on, Bo. Get with it. This is it, a chance of a lifetime."

It was tempting. God, was it tempting. I'd actually be with him for four or five or even six weeks. There was not only a book in it there was a movie in it. Hell two books, two movies, and a one-man Broadway show that would run forever. All I had to do was say yes, or nod, or slap my hands on the table and say, "damn right."

For a second I was having trouble breathing. It was all happening too fast. If I'd had any warning I would have been able to deal with it. But this was much too quick, much too sudden, and I couldn't catch up. His arm was around my shoulder, he was talking about the night games and the crowds that loved him and how they had never been able to get enough of Satchel Paige and the Satchel Paige All-Stars.

And then I knew where I'd seen the scene before. It was *Pinocchio*. All I had to do was say "maybe" and the fiddle music would start. We'd sing "Hi-Diddle-de-dee-an-actor's-life-for-me. . . ." Then I'd leap up against the cartoon moon and click my heels and throw away my cares and we'd start tap dancing across the Kentucky Fried Chicken parking lot. And then Satch would laugh and roar like Mister Bones and he'd leap higher and click his heels faster and laugh louder and we'd sing the second verse together. Then, arm in arm, we'd go cakewalking down the silver-spangled white line into the tangerine moon and fame and riches and our names in lights that would burn forever. All we needed were top hats and gold walking canes. All we needed were silver pants and phosphorescent vests and rhinestone dagger shoes. All I had to do was say yes.

Even today I don't know why I said I had too much to do back in L.A. and couldn't go. But as I said it I knew I was lying. I'd turned into just another Charley. And like Charley I'd ducked my head and gone shuffling back to my nine-to-five world. But I could have gone, I should have gone, and ever since that night I've been kicking my ass for not going and wondering why I didn't.

But Satch understood and in a minute he had Clete in the front seat instead of me and had the car started and was ready to leave the lot and head west. We said goodbye and he grinned and soft-punched my shoulder, "You hold her in the road now, you hear?"

"OK, Satch. I'll do what I can. You be good now."

As he pulled out, with the car framed in the bottom of the red rolling moon, he raised his hand as high as he could reach and waved back hollering, "So long, Bo." And then he was gone.

Now, almost thirty years later, whenever I think of his laugh, his lies and stories, his extravagant untamed character, and the unbelievable ricochet echo he's left behind, I see that same moon shining down that same road, and then it comes as it always does and always will, the same old tears.

POSTSCRIPT

OF ALL THE things I've written, I'm now sure this is my favorite. It's not a novel or a biography, as a matter of cold fact I don't think I know what it is. At first I thought it would make a good two-man stage show, with someone playing Satch and someone setting him up, or a one-man show with someone like Morgan Freeman just sitting up on stage and rambling away. Then I thought it would make a very good full-length musical set in the thirties and forties when the Negro Baseball League was in its prime. Then I didn't know what I thought. A couple agents and editors didn't know either, but as they say in the trade they're the last people to know anything.

Now I could have shaped this into a novel, but then I decided against that because I really didn't want to make Satch anything other than what he was. All I knew was I wanted to get him on some kind of stage and see where it went from there—which is precisely what I wound up doing. The funny part is I did just that but at the time I didn't have a clue to what I was doing or where it was going. Does that make any sense? In the end I just kept him talking and tried to pick up his great voice and wonderful sound and the incredible humor he brought to his stories and almost everything he said.

When I met Satch for the first time in the Twilight Zone Lounge of the Rhythm Lanes Bowling Alley (God, I still love the sound of that), the first thing he told me was he'd been stopped by the police in Columbia, S.C., my hometown, on suspicion of hauling illegal whiskey. So what we did right there was start talking about the corn whiskey business. I was lucky here because I can hold the floor with anyone on this. My dad and his two brothers, M. L. and Chauncey, were moonshiners who designed and built stills and made it back in the swamps. They were also bootleggers who drove it into town and sold it, and finally state and federal prisoners for being caught with it.

When I wound down he played a few cards about how back in Mississippi when he was a kid he'd help run a "groundhog still" and sold whiskey bottles to the bootleggers. I dragged the pot when I told him about Dad holding up a waffle-ridged pint bottle and proclaiming "a man or a woman can drink my whiskey from this bottle standing in the rain and not have to worry about dropping it."

Anyhow, we went back and forth with corn whiskey stories until finally Jay Cee Bee, the editor of the *Kansas City Call*, who wanted the conversation to stay on a higher level, interrupted with, "Satch, what do you consider your greatest contribution to baseball?" Satch shook his head in true disappointment. "Shhhh-eet, J. C., what kind of question is that? Why don't you just get on out of here and let me and Bo talk."

Well for a solid week we talked; at the Twilight Zone Lounge, Gates's Barbecue, the Flamingo Club, the Club Oasis, the Muhlebach Hotel, Satch's home, the Midas Muffler Shop, and out at the park where he was warming up getting ready to go out on the road on a barnstorming tour.

One of the best decisions I've ever made was not to tape Satch or take any notes while he was talking. Later I found out that if I taped him he went flat and ordinary and almost uninteresting. And if I took notes, he'd read what I was writing and start editing himself and do the same thing. Satch was about a lot of things, but what I thought, and still think, was the most important and most revealing was his voice, his sounds, his delivery. I can't think of anyone except Richard Pryor doing his Madame Dubose and the Mojo Woman that even comes close.

I read somewhere that a musicologist once said he could hear one single note from Louis Armstrong and know it was him. Satch was that distinct and that different. A lot of us can recognize Faulkner or Flannery O'Connor or Jane Austen or Dylan Thomas by a single line or a couple of lines. But Satch not only had his own voice and rhythm, he could go high or low, shade it, speed it up or slow it down to a dead crawl and watch it roll over. He could also imitate at least a dozen people. Not only could he imitate their voices, he'd show you the way they stood and walked and laughed. When he imitated Casey Stengel warning his Yankee batters to get their hits as soon as possible because Satch, then playing for Cleveland, was coming in in relief he'd put on a whole show. He'd cock his hat down low on his nose like Stengel, hunch over and walk bowlegged back and forth like a chicken. He'd spit in the dirt and kick it and tell them, "All right now, when Father Time starts pitching he ain't going to give you nothing. Nothing. So you got to get me them hits now. I mean now. Right now. I want me them hits now."

Satch could go from Casey Stengel to Lou Boudreau to Dizzy Dean to Earl and Huey Long and every voice would be absolutely on the money. For Jelly Roll Morton he went into a sharp, classy but slightly sleazy Creole, snapping his fingers and using long finger pulls as he slid in and out of songs Jelly Roll was playing that year.

One thing I left out of the book was how the customers at the nightclubs and Gates's Barbecue gathered around him just to touch him on the arm or shoulder. Later someone told me they loved him so much they just had to do it. Some thought part of his magic would rub off on them. Martin Luther King Jr. and Mohammed Ali had the same effect on people.

Of course there's another side to Satch's life when you read about him. Many of the writers simply copied what had already been written and exaggerated lines that he'd never said. Their stories all sounded the same because they were the same. One enterprising national magazine published Satch's "Rules for Living," which he had nothing to do with. One of the rules was "Never eat anything fried. Fried foods angrify the blood." I covered this in the book and have him turning over every rock.

I didn't realize what an effect Satch's voice and character had on me until I was writing my novel *Dixiana Moon*. One of the characters, Buck Mozingo, a circus owner and hustler, was telling someone how bad the Depression was. "One day I saw a big rat sitting on a trash can and that rat was eating an onion. And that rat was crying. I mean tears like you and me cry. Human tears. So I said to myself if a rat can't make out any better than that we're really in some trouble here." Satch didn't say that but he could have. I also did an all-black musical here in Columbia with Franklin Ashley and Shel Silverstein and a lot of Satch came through there too.

A lot of Satch's voice and character is still ringing in my head where it's been for a long, long time now. And what I'm going to do is make damn sure it never leaves.